The Philosophy of
Derrida

Continental European Philosophy

This series provides accessible and stimulating introductions to the ideas of continental thinkers who have shaped the fundamentals of European philosophical thought. Powerful and radical, the ideas of these philosophers have often been contested, but they remain key to understanding current philosophical thinking as well as the current direction of disciplines such as political science, literary theory, comparative literature, art history, and cultural studies. Each book seeks to combine clarity with depth, introducing fresh insights and wider perspectives while also providing a comprehensive survey of each thinker's philosophical ideas.

Published titles

The Philosophy of Derrida
Mark Dooley and Liam Kavanagh

The Philosophy of Kierkegaard
George Pattison

The Philosophy of Foucault
Todd May

The Philosophy of Merleau-Ponty
Eric Matthews

The Philosophy of Gadamer
Jean Grondin

The Philosophy of Nietzsche
Rex Welshon

The Philosophy of Habermas
Andrew Edgar

The Philosophy of Schopenhauer
Dale Jacquette

Forthcoming titles include

The Philosophy of Hegel
Allen Speight

The Philosophy of Kant
Jim O'Shea

The Philosophy of Husserl
Burt Hopkins

The Philosophy of Sartre
Anthony Hatzimoysis

The Philosophy of Derrida

*Mark Dooley and
Liam Kavanagh*

McGill-Queen's University Press
Montreal & Kingston • Ithaca

© Mark Dooley and Liam Kavanagh 2007

ISBN 978-0-7735-3234-2 (bound)
ISBN 978-0-7735-3235-9 (pbk.)

Legal deposit first quarter 2007
Bibliothèque nationale du Québec

Published simultaneously outside North America
by Acumen Publishing Limited

McGill-Queen's University Press acknowledges the financial support of
the Government of Canada through the Book Publishing Development
Program (bpidp) for its activities.

Library and Archives Canada Cataloguing in Publication

Dooley, Mark
    The philosophy of Derrida / Mark Dooley and Liam Kavanagh.

(Continental European philosophy)
Includes bibliographical references and index.
ISBN 978-0-7735-3234-2 (bound)
ISBN 978-0-7735-3235-9 (pbk.)

    1. Derrida, Jacques. 2. Identity (Philosophical concept). 3. Memory--
Philosophy. I. Kavanagh, Liam, 1973- II. Title. III. Series.

B2430.D484D66 2007   194   C2006-905658-7

Designed and typeset by Kate Williams, Swansea.
Printed and bound by Cromwell Press, Trowbridge.

Contents

Preface

This book has two aims. First, it attempts to bring clarity to the philosophy of Jacques Derrida. Secondly, it does so by arguing that he is fundamentally concerned with the related questions of memory and identity. Our central assertion is that misunderstandings of Derrida arise because of his obscure prose style, and because few commentators have tried to draw out an underlying theme in his work. We contend that his diverse writings do contain such a theme, and that it gives them continuity and structure.

In short, this book argues that, like Plato and Hegel before him, Jacques Derrida believes that a human being's identity is built on memory. When we think about our historical origins we rely on memory to recollect whence we came. For Plato that means recalling the true nature of the self in the immaterial world of the Forms. For Hegel it means dialectically recovering the self through the various stages of consciousness. But in both cases the objective is to overcome alienation by achieving full self-awareness. Self-identity, in other words, means reclaiming our origins through the use of memory.

For Derrida, however, recovering the self from the manifold layers of time and history is much more complex than Plato, Hegel or indeed most philosophers are prepared to concede. And despite the notorious difficulties encountered by those attempting to read him, his point is simple: we are from the beginning of existence situated at the end of a multilayered web of beliefs and practices. As such, there is no way we can comprehensively unstitch the various folds of history that precede us. Yes, historical memory can provide us with a sense of who we are and whence we came, but it is incapable of bringing us face to face with every historical occurrence. The reason for that is also simple: memory does not correspond to the reality of the past, but merely traces a partial outline of what went before. That means the process of self-recollection is impossible for Derrida, simply because memory can never make the past fully present.

What Derrida challenges, therefore, is the classic metaphysical assumption that self-identity, or self-presence, can be achieved through historical recollection. Identity is predicated on memory, and because memory fundamentally fails to deliver, we can never be absolutely certain of who we are. That is what he calls "the catastrophe of memory". If the philosophical tradition assumed self-presence is a given, Derrida shows that the self is always already disjointed, unhinged and unable to completely retrace itself through the vicissitudes of time.

What this suggests is that Derrida's philosophy, commonly known as deconstruction, strives to show that any construct – philosophical, theological, scientific – claiming to have pure access to our beginnings is mistaken. Deconstruction, in other words, is an assault on the notion of purity. By showing that all constructs are predicated on a multitude of texts and traces, and because all texts and traces are subject to the catastrophe of memory, all constructs can therefore be deconstructed. In sum, they cannot deliver us from alienation to the satisfaction of self-presence. That is not to say, however, that they cannot bring us some of the way towards self-harmony. But it does imply that philosophical, theological or scientific structures are not pure all the way down. And that is because, like everything else, they have a history.

If looked at from this perspective, the philosophy of Jacques Derrida is neither radical nor iconoclastic. It agrees with Plato and Hegel that philosophical reflection is primarily about self-identity. It also supports their view that identity and memory are inextricably intertwined. Where it departs from their analysis is on the question of how productive memory is in recapturing what is lost from present consciousness. Derrida, that is, takes seriously the critiques of classical metaphysics by Søren Kierkegaard and Friedrich Nietzsche. Their belief that we are unable to assume a God's-eye standpoint beyond time and history is at the heart of deconstruction. Consequently, deconstruction owes a significant debt to existentialism. All three thinkers deny the belief that history is developmental: that it has a beginning, middle and end. "Fundamentally," says Derrida, "Kierkegaard, Nietzsche and others are thinkers of the untimely, who begin by putting into question the interpretation of history as development, in which something that is contemporary to itself – self-contemporary – can succeed something that is past" (TS: 6).

Chapter 1 of this book will tease out the question of memory in Derrida's work. It will relate it to the no less important theme of mourning. Derrida makes it clear that because of the catastrophe of memory, deconstruction is a "work of mourning". Whereas for Hegel memory or consciousness is capable of resurrecting the past, Derrida does not believe that such a resurrection is possible. That is why he mourns for a past that can never be brought back to life, or can never be, as Hegel would say, dialectically sub-sumed by consciousness. It is also why Derrida is preoccupied in his writings by death, ghosts and spirits. They exist for him because the past can never be fully made present and laid to rest.

In Chapter 2, we show how these themes of identity, loss, memory and mourning function in Derrida's philosophy of language. By showing how speech is always haunted from within by writing or traces, we make sense of Derrida's controversial claim that "there is nothing outside the text". We also analyse his confrontation with the analytic tradition of language philosophy, especially in the guise of J. L. Austin, John Searle and W. V. O. Quine.

Chapter 3 focuses on the traditions of phenomenology and psychoanaly-sis from which Derrida drew much of his early inspiration. We show how his writings on Sigmund Freud, Edmund Husserl and Martin Heidegger are no less concerned with memory and identity. We also highlight the fact that while these thinkers each display deconstructive tendencies, they ulti-mately fail to bring those tendencies to fruition. Whereas Freud, Husserl and Heidegger are thinkers of history, they do not, in the final analysis, make sufficient room for death and real mourning.

Chapter 4 deals with Derrida's recent writings on ethics and politics. While we maintain that Derrida is first and foremost an ethical thinker, his work became more ethically explicit in the decade preceding his death in 2004. Here we dwell on his theories of law, justice and hospitality. We also discuss Richard Rorty's contention that Derrida is a private philosopher devoid of concrete political significance. We conclude that while there are indeed instances where Derrida failed to meet his own criteria of what Der-ridean justice demands, he was ultimately neither a private nor a public phi-losopher as defined by Rorty. And, despite his latter-day admiration for Karl Marx, he was no radical or reactionary. In the end, Derrida was someone who sought to preserve the best of our philosophical, scientific, religious and political traditions. That is what he meant by "the work of mourning". But he did so with an eye to novelty and justice, repetition and love. As such, he was a philosopher in the tradition of Socrates and Hegel, thinkers whose questioning of tradition never compromised their love for it.

Derrida left an indelible mark on the contemporary intellectual land-scape. He was both adored and reviled in equal measure. But behind all the controversy lay a simple idea: full self-understanding is impossible because we cannot roll back the layers of time and history that precede us to reveal our origins in their purity. It is a pity that Derrida's unnecessarily difficult and nebulous style obscured that basic point. This book hopes to redress that by making explicit what lay implicitly at the heart of all Derrida's works.

Abbreviations

A   *Aporias*, Thomas Dutoit (trans.) (Stanford, CA: Stanford University Press, 1993).

AF   *Archive Fever: A Freudian Impression*, Eric Prenowitz (trans.) (Chicago, IL: University of Chicago Press, 1995).

C   *Circumfession: Fifty-nine Periods and Periphrases*, in Geoffrey Bennington & Jacques Derrida, *Jacques Derrida* (Chicago, IL: University of Chicago Press, 1993).

CS   *Cinders*, Ned Lukacher (trans.) (Lincoln, NE: University of Nebraska Press, 1991).

D   *Dissemination*, Barbara Johnson (trans.) (Chicago, IL: University of Chicago Press, 1981).

DO   "Deconstruction and the Other", in *Debates in Continental Philosophy: Conversations with Contemporary Thinkers*, Richard Kearney, 139–56 (New York: Fordham University Press, 2004).

EO   *The Ear of the Other*, Peggy Kamuf (trans.) (Lincoln, NE: University of Nebraska Press, 1985).

ET   *Echographies of Television*, Jacques Derrida & Bernard Stiegler (Cambridge: Polity, 2002).

FoL   "Force of Law: The 'Mystical Foundation of Authority'", in *Deconstruction and the Possibility of Justice*, Drucilla Cornell (ed.), 3–67 (New York: Routledge, 1992).

FWT   *For What Tomorrow … A Dialogue*, Jacques Derrida & Elisabeth Roundinesco, Jeff Fort (trans.) (Stanford, CA: Stanford University Press, 2004.

G   *Glas*, Richard Rand & John Leavey (trans.) (Lincoln, NE: University of Nebraska Press, 1986).

GD   *The Gift of Death*, David Wills (trans.) (Chicago, IL: University of Chicago Press, 1995).

GT   *Given Time. I. Counterfeit Money*, Peggy Kamuf (trans.) (Chicago, IL: University of Chicago Press, 1991).

H   "Hospitality, Justice and Responsibility: A Dialogue with Jacques Derrida", in *Questioning Ethics*, Richard Kearney & Mark Dooley (eds), 65–83 (London: Routledge, 1999).

LI   *Limited Inc.*, Samuel Weber (trans.) (Evanston, IL: Northwestern University Press, 2000).

M   *Margins of Philosophy*, Alan Bass (trans.) (Chicago, IL: University of Chicago Press, 1982).

MB   *Memoirs of the Blind: The Self-Portrait and Other Ruins*, Pascale-Anne Brault & Michael Naas (trans.) (Chicago, IL: University of Chicago Press, 1993).

MdP *Mémoires: For Paul de Man*, Cecile Lindsay, Jonathan Culler & Eduardo Cadava (trans.) (New York: Columbia University Press, 1986).

MO *Monolingualism of the Other: The Prosthesis of Origin* (Stanford, CA: Stanford University Press, 1998).

MS "Marx & Sons", G. M. Goshgarian (trans.), in *Ghostly Demarcations: A Symposium on Jacques Derrida's Specters of Marx*, Michael Sprinker (ed.), 213–69 (London: Verso, 1999).

N *Negotiations: Interventions and Interviews, 1971–2001* (Stanford, CA: Stanford University Press, 2002).

OC *On Cosmopolitanism and Forgiveness*, Mark Dooley & Michael Hughes (trans.) (London: Routledge, 2001).

OG *Of Grammatology*, Gayatri Spivak (trans.) (Baltimore, MD: Johns Hopkins University Press, 1974).

OH *Of Hospitality*, Rachel Bowlby (trans.) (Stanford, CA: Stanford University Press, 2000).

OS *Of Spirit: Heidegger and the Question*, Geoffrey Bennington & Rachel Bowlby (trans.) (Chicago, IL: University of Chicago Press, 1987).

P *Points ... Interviews, 1974–94*, Elisabeth Weber (ed.), Peggy Kamuf *et al.* (trans.) (Stanford, CA: Stanford University Press, 1995).

PC *The Post Card: From Socrates to Freud and Beyond*, Alan Bass (trans.) (Chicago, IL: University of Chicago Press, 1987).

PF "Politics and Friendship: A Discussion with Jacques Derrida", www.sussex.ac.uk/Units/frenchthought/derrida.htm (accessed September 2006).

PI "Psyche: Inventions of the Other", in *Reading de Man Reading*, Lindsay Waters & Wlad Godzich, 25–65 (Minneapolis, MN: University of Minnesota Press, 1989).

Pos *Positions*, Alan Bass (trans.) (Chicago, IL: University of Chicago Press, 1972).

PT *Philosophy in a Time of Terror: Dialogues with Jurgen Habermas and Jacques Derrida*, Giovanna Borradori (ed.) (Chicago, IL: University of Chicago Press, 2003).

R *Rogues: Two Essays On Reason*, Pascale-Anne Brault & Michael Naas (trans.) (Stanford, CA: Stanford University Press, 2005).

RDP "Remarks on Deconstruction and Pragmatism", in *Deconstruction and Pragmatism*, C. Mouffe (ed.), 77–88 (London: Routledge, 1996).

Res. *Resistances of Psychoanalysis*, Peggy Kamuf, Pascale-Anne Brault, & Michael Naas (trans.) (Stanford, CA: Stanford University Press, 1998).

S "Shibboleth: For Paul Celan", in *Sovereignties in Question: The Poetics of Paul Celan*, Thomas Dutoit & Outi Pasanen (eds), Joshua Wilner (trans.), 1–64 (New York: Fordham University Press, 2005).

SEC "Signature Event Context", in *Margins of Philosophy* (M), 309–30.

SM *Specters of Marx: The State of the Debt, the Work of Mourning, and the New International*, Peggy Kamuf (trans.) (New York: Routledge, 1994).

SP *Speech and Phenomena and Other Essays on Husserl's Theory of Signs*, David Allison (trans.) (Evanston, IL: Northwestern University Press, 1973).

TS *A Taste for the Secret*, Jacques Derrida & Maurizio Ferraris, Giacoma Donis (trans.) (Cambridge: Polity, 2002).

TT "The Time of the Thesis: Punctuation", in *Philosophy in France Today*, Alan Montefiore (ed.), 34–50 (Cambridge: Cambridge University Press, 1983).

VR "The Villanova Roundtable", in *Deconstruction in a Nutshell: A Conversation with Jacques Derrida*, John D. Caputo, 3–28 (New York: Fordham University Press, 1997).

WD *Writing and Difference*, Alan Bass (trans.) (Chicago, IL: University of Chicago Press, 1978).
WM *The Work of Mourning*, Pascale-Anne Brault & Michael Naas (eds) (Chicago, IL: University of Chicago Press, 2001).
YV "An Interview with Professor Jacques Derrida", www1.yadvashem.org/odot_pdf/ Microsoft%20Word%20-%203851.pdf (accessed October 2006).

CHAPTER ONE

The catastrophe of memory: identity and mourning

Identity and belonging

On the first day of school in 1942, the twelve-year-old Jacques Derrida was expelled from the Lycée de Ben Aknoun, near El-Biar in Algeria. Two years previously, in October 1940, the French citizenship that had formerly been granted to Algerian Jews by the Crémieux Decree of 1870 was abruptly withdrawn. And when segregation laws were subsequently introduced in Algeria in March 1941, all Jews were prohibited from working in the liberal professions, and Jewish children were expelled from elementary and secondary schools to meet segregationist quotas. The decision by the Vichy administration at once denied the Jewish community their right to citizenship and identity, while cynically unleashing the officially sanctioned anti-Semitism that followed. Without warning or explanation, the young "Jackie" Derrida, "a little black and very Arab Jew" (C: 58), suddenly found himself exposed to the violent trauma of exclusion and non-belonging.

The memory of this event would have a profound effect on the young Derrida. Henceforth, he had no sense of self. He had neither language nor tradition, and was an exile in his own community, a fact highlighted in the following reflection:

> From that moment, I felt – how to put it? – just as out-of-place in a closed Jewish community as I did on the other side (we called them "the Catholics"). In France, the suffering subsided. At nineteen, I naively thought that anti-Semitism had disappeared, at least there where I was living at the time. But during adolescence, it was the tragedy, it was present in everything else … Paradoxical effect, perhaps, of this brutalization: a desire but painful and suspicious desire, nervously vigilant, an exhausting aptitude to detect signs of racism, in its most discreet configurations or its noisiest disavowals.

1

> Symmetrically, sometimes, an impatient distance with regard to the Jewish communities, whenever I have the impression that they are closing themselves off by posing themselves as such. Whence a feeling of non-belonging that I have no doubt transposed ...   (P: 121)

Those early experiences of detachment and non-belonging permeate Derrida's entire philosophical endeavour. And that is because he was forced to recognize that identity is not something concrete and certain. Rather, it is a complex web containing within itself multiple layers that cannot easily be unravelled. As he asks, "what is identity, this concept of which the transparent identity to itself is always dogmatically presupposed by so many debates in monoculturalism or multiculturalism, nationality, citizenship, and, in general, belonging?" (MO: 14). In other words, do geographical borders, shared languages, traditions or currencies determine one's personal or national identity? When, for example, these borders expand and contract, or when traditional "European" values are influenced by values from other cultures, does the identity of Europe itself change?

In 1942, to be "French" was predicated on not being an Algerian Jew. And that was not a matter of mere semantics. The subtle shift in the determination of French identity resulted in very real acts of violence. So, just as his own identity was marked by the memory of difference and non-belonging, Derrida argues that all of our traditional values, customs and institutions conceal repressed acts of violence and exclusion. That being said, it is not our traditional ideals, values and institutions *themselves* that Derrida finds problematic; rather, it is the particular *form* of identity they presuppose. In other words, they are structured by what Derrida calls the logic of "presence", or "logocentrism".

Presence and loss

In one of his most celebrated essays, "Structure, Sign and Play in the Discourse of the Human Sciences", Derrida writes "that all the names related to fundamentals, to principles, or to the center have always designated an invariable presence – *eidos, archē, telos, energeia, ousia* (essence, existence, substance, subject) *alētheia*, transcendentality, consciousness, God, man and so forth" (WD: 279–80). This typically obscure Derridean sentence simply means that identity has traditionally implied purity and wholeness. To identify with someone or something means to have a full knowledge of that person or object. As such, knowledge admits of no black spots or inaccessible dimensions. What we identify with is completely present to consciousness.

2

Things are never that simple, however. The identity of a person or thing always conceals something from view. Part of what we are endeavouring to understand defies our longing to make it transparent. And the reason for that is that everything has a long and convoluted history that cannot be rendered fully present. While I can try to understand a person or an object by unstitching its history, I cannot fully recreate its actual temporal experience. We can try our best to comprehend the thoughts and life of another person, but we can never make them absolutely present to us. Even the act of perception is always incomplete. We can only perceive things from limited angles and perspectives. Something will always evade speculative comprehension.

That is why Derrida never wrote an autobiography. In fact, he did not believe such a thing was possible. The nearest he came to writing a personal memoir was a book he co-wrote with Geoffrey Bennington entitled, *Jacques Derrida* (1993). On the top half of each page, Bennington attempted an exhaustive analysis of Derrida's work. On the bottom, Derrida contributed "fifty-nine periods and periphrases", which he called "Circumfession". That, of course, is a play on the word "circumcision" or the original cut. Derrida's confession about his life and times is, in other words, incomplete. It is a confession that is circumcised. And it is so because, as he asserts, no human being can fully recover the manifold layers of history that make up a life. Each of us is cut from our origins by time and what Derrida calls "the catastrophe of memory":

> I would say that what I suffer from inconsolably always has the form, not only of loss, which is often! – but of the loss of memory: that what I am living not be kept, thus repeated, and – how to put it? – decipherable, as if an appeal for a witness had no witness, in some way, not even the witness that I could be for what I have lived. This is for me the very experience of death, of catastrophe.
>
> (P: 207)

The catastrophe of memory renders autobiography impossible. With the passing of each and every second, time ravages the present. And what we are left with is a past incapable of being completely recollected.[1] Hence we have Derrida's refusal to write a conventional autobiography. Instead, he gives us elusive fragments representing patchy and incomplete memory, which are totally at odds with Bennington's philosophical biography at the top of the page.[2]

The time is out of joint

Derrida cannot write an autobiography because he is, to cite Julia Kristeva, a stranger to himself. The name "Jacques Derrida" symbolizes a history that is haunted from within by secrets and ghosts, none of which can be made fully present to him or us. And the same goes for every person, thing and institution. This accounts for why he opposes the idea of history as a comprehensive process in which the past is gathered up and rendered fully present. On Derrida's account, history is not linear, developmental, logical or coherent. Due to the fact that it contains within itself gaps and secrets, ghosts and holes, it can never tell us who we are. If identity is dependent on history, and if history is founded on faulty memory, then identity is without origin or foundation. And if that is so, then it follows we are always "dislocated" from ourselves. Derrida explains:

> "The time is out of joint," says Hamlet. Literally, "to be out of joint" is said of a shoulder or a knee that has gone out of its socket that is dislocated, disjointed. Thus, time "out of joint" is time outside itself, beside itself, unhinged; it is not gathered together in its place, in its present. (TS: 6)

All time and history is out of joint. It is simply impossible, given the catastrophe of memory, to adjust time in such a way that all its component parts can be gathered up harmoniously. For, to repeat, no matter how hard we try we cannot re-enact historical events in their fullness. Each event is a singular experience that vanishes into memory. And once that happens, the singularity of that experience is lost forever, retained only in spectral form; which is why, for Derrida, the possibility of any identity is its simultaneous impossibility. In other words, everything has a history, and because it is impossible to give a complete account of that history there can be no such thing as pure identity. The very possibility of the painting of a landscape, for example, is simultaneously the impossibility of that painting capturing every possible detail. And just as the painting is a partial or incomplete encapsulation, so too history is an incomplete encapsulation of the past. There will always be something that has escaped the artist's and the historian's gaze. What Derrida calls the "unity of identity" is thus shattered from within.

> As for the dream of unity … this dream is forever destined to disappointment; this unity remains inaccessible; that does not mean that the dream is but a fantasy, imaginary, a secondary moment …
>
> Even if this dream is destined to remain a dream, the promise – it is better to speak of promise rather than dream – the promise,

as promise, is an event, it exists; there is the promise of unity and that is what sets desire in motion; there is desire.   (P: 136)

If the dream of unity is destined to disappointment, however, that does not and must not prevent us from endeavouring to recreate the past or to write biography. While unity and complete recollection are impossible, the dream or promise of unity is what drives us to undertake historical research; it is still the driving force behind our quest for meaning and identity. All passion, and all hopes for a better future, presuppose this incompleteness of desire.

From Derrida's point of view, the task of the historian is to acknowledge that while retrieving historical contexts in their purity is impossible, we must still make decisions regarding how to make history coherent. That is a task for the imagination and creative impulse of the historian. And because filling in memory's gaps is a highly speculative and uncertain exercise, it is an endless enterprise. This is what Derrida means when he says, "what we call the opening of the [historical] context is another name for what is still to come" (TS: 20).

Memory and mastery

Once a historical context is consumed by memory, it contains secrets that elude excavation. As a result, "the context is not absolutely determinable: there is a context but one cannot analyze it exhaustively" (TS: 13). The singularity of experience itself, of my lived experience, is something that defies and resists repetition. The lived moment is unique and singular because it can never be repeated exactly as it happened in the past.[3] But, according to Derrida, trying to repeat and recollect the singularity of past events and contexts is precisely the vocation philosophy has assumed for itself. Philosophers have always aspired to this sense of mastery over the past, this attempt to capture everything without remainder:

> The philosopher is someone whose desire and ambition are absolutely mad; the desire for power of the greatest politicians is absolutely minuscule and juvenile compared to the desire of the philosopher who, in a philosophical work, manifests both a design on mastery and a renunciation of mastery on a scale and to a degree that I find infinitely more powerful than can be found elsewhere, for example, with the great politicians or military men, or those who have economic power at their disposal.   (P: 139)

5

Philosophers, however, have traditionally failed to take account of the fact that this desire to master the past is destined to fail. Instead of acknowledging the catastrophe of memory, "philosophy, or academic philosophy at any rate, for me has always been at the service of this autobiographical design of memory". And that autobiographical design of memory – what Derrida refers to as "memoirs" – is "the wild desire to preserve everything, to gather everything together in its idiom" (TS: 41). Whether in the name of the Good, God or Universal Spirit, philosophers always attempt to gather everything round a single organizing centre, assigning everything its proper place and leaving nothing unaccounted for. This is why, for Derrida, our traditional understanding of identity, history and memory always assumes the form of a circle: an "Odyssean structure", whereby everything "would always follow the path of Ulysses ... that of an economy and a nostalgia, a 'homesickness,' a provisional exile and longing for reappropriation" (GT: 6–7). Historical memory, for example, always begins with an original presence or lived event that is temporarily deferred, only to be recollected again at a later stage. Like Ulysses, the historian follows this circular path in an attempt to return home and relive the past.

The figure of the circle is at the heart of Derrida's critique of the philosophical tradition, and recurs again and again throughout his texts. Since *The Post Card* (PC) in which he traces the circular movement of letters in the post, to his analysis of writing, intentionality and the archive, to the circular cut of circumcision, Derrida continually discerns in the philosophical tradition the attempt to gather all identity and memory within the safe enclosure of a circle. But if historical memory follows the movement of a circle, then the catastrophe of memory testifies to the fact that the circle can never be complete. Like the mark of circumcision, the circle is always cut. We are always cut and detached from our past. Unlike Ulysses, who always finds his way back, we are like Abraham, exiled from his place of birth, endlessly *destin-errant*, wandering the desert in search of a home. And because time cuts and dislocates me from my past, leaving only traces of what was once present, I am to a certain extent blind. Memory robs me of sight, in as much as I cannot bring the past fully into view. As such, all memoirs are by their very nature "memoirs of the blind".[4] I simply cannot see the past in its purity or presence. And what is concealed from view is "not a thing, some information that I am hiding or that one has to hide or dissimulate; it is rather an experience that does not make itself available to information, that resists information and knowledge, and that immediately encrypts itself" (P: 201).

Cinders and mourning

The point here is that what the past hides from view, what escapes the closure of the circle, is not something that awaits retrieval or exposure. It is not a secret in the conventional sense, where information is being shielded from view only to be recalled or discovered at some future date. What is hidden, according to Derrida, is irretrievably lost. That is why he says that the catastrophe of memory is an "experience of death". The fact that I cannot write an autobiography means that self-presence or identity is shattered from within by death. As each moment passes, something of myself dies. Sometimes what is lost is partially retained in written, oral or pictorial form. But there are many moments that simply disappear without a trace, or without any testimony whatsoever. Such is what Derrida calls the "experience of cinders":

> I would be reconciled with everything I live, even the worst things, if I were assured that the memory of it would stay with me, or stay as well as the testimony that gives meaning or that brings to light, that permits the thing to reappear. The experience of cinders is the experience not only of forgetting, but of the forgetting of forgetting, of the forgetting of which nothing remains. (P: 207)

Cinders or ashes are traces of a disintegrated past, consumed by the fires of time. They are "something that remains without remaining, which is neither present nor absent, which destroys itself, which is totally consumed, which is a remainder without remainder" (P: 208). Cinders symbolize the remains of something that was formerly present but is now dead. While they bear witness to the existence of something, they never reveal what that something was. It is impossible, in other words, to reconstruct what once was from a pile of cinders. Hence, they testify "to the disappearance of memory" or "to the destruction of memory itself" (P: 208–9). And that experience of destruction or death is, according to Derrida, at the heart of all experience:

> to say that there are cinders there [il y a là cendre] … is to say that in every trace, in every writing, and consequently in every experience (for me every experience is, in a certain way, an experience of trace and writing), in every experience there is this incineration, this experience of incineration which is experience itself. (P: 209)

In short, we are cut from our origins, blinded to our past, and incapable of writing an autobiography, because the present is haunted from within by traces and cinders. Death and loss are at the heart of all identity and experience. Which is why, for Derrida, an act of memory, the desire to identify with the past, is always a work of mourning: "the only motif or motive that would be proper to me" (P: 48). We mourn the fact that we can never resurrect the past, but this should not be cause for sorrow and regret. The past may be irretrievably lost, but that does not prevent us from attempting to resurrect it. Cinders may testify to the impossibility of recollection, but that does not mean that we do not do our best to interpret them. If memory testifies to the fact that we can never fully recollect the past, then mourning affirms that we are never finished with the past: that the task of comprehending the past always lies ahead of us.

When a loved one dies, for example, we know that we can never resurrect them as they were; we can never bring them back. We are forever at the mercy of traces when trying to recover the past. We are never in a position to fully recreate what or who has gone before. For example, I can tell you about the life of my great-grandfather based on stories, images and written testament. But however hard I try I shall never fill in all the gaps and bring him back to life. And even if I had a video recording of every moment of his life, it would still only be a partial testimony of the flesh-and-blood life. All I really have to go on are disjointed remnants that are adjusted by me in order to establish a coherent narrative. But that, of course, does not mean that because there are only traces of my great-grandfather in existence, I will not try to recreate his life. While memory might fail us, mourning will inspire us to try the impossible and bring him back to life. Naturally, we shall not succeed. But that will only prompt us into further research to find out more about the life we are trying to recover. In short, it is the impossible act of endeavouring to infuse the past with life – to make it present, or bring it home to us – that makes us passionate about historical investigation. It is, in other words, unavoidable loss that drives us to mourn the past and, in so doing, attempt the impossible by resurrecting it. Our loved ones may be irretrievably lost, but when we mourn we continue to keep them with us and offer them the possibility of a future. We keep them with us to the extent that we continue to tell their stories, to share pictures, recollections and memories. Even in death we are always still getting to know them. The dead are never completely departed. There are always traces, cinders and remains that continue to haunt, disturb and inspire us.

We do not mourn, therefore, only in times of bereavement. If all identity is historical, then all historical analysis is a work of mourning. The historian can never simply recollect or have a complete knowledge of the past. As in *Circumfession*, he can only attempt to stitch together and interpret the many cinders and traces of memory. But if the catastrophe of memory testifies to the impossibility of recollecting the past, then the work of mourning, while accepting that we must let go of our claims to mastery, nonetheless desires to keep and preserve it, and give it new life. Like the charred remains of a photograph, the work of mourning bears witness to a past that can never again be made present, but that nonetheless demands of us that its story be told. We can never resurrect the past from the ashes of history. But in mourning we still strive to interpret it and make it coherent, to do our best to tell its story and give it the promise of a future.

The gift

The attempt to recollect and gather the past into a harmonious whole always follows the path of a circular economy. Economy, from the Greek *oikonomia*, has its origin in the words *oikos* (home) and *nomos* (law). Economy is literally the law or management (*nemein*) of one's home. It is the means by which we strive to return home and recreate the past. But the work of mourning testifies to the fact that this circle can never come to completion: that we can never return home. Derrida illustrates both the circular movement of economy as well as the work of mourning that strives to resist it, in terms of the logic of the gift.

We are all familiar with the everyday activity of giving and receiving gifts whereby someone gives something to someone else. According to Derrida, however, a pure gift can never be presented. As soon as a gift is presented by one person to another, an obligation is imposed on the recipient to reciprocate the generosity of the donor, by returning a gift that equals or exceeds in value the original offering. The donor always re-collects what he or she has lost from the original act of giving through an economic payback from the donee. And even if the donor does not want any payback, even if they genuinely desire to give a gift unconditionally – "with no strings attached" – as soon as it is recognized by the recipient *as* a gift, it is immediately drawn into this economy of exchange.

We therefore find ourselves caught in a peculiar bind. We desire to give gifts unconditionally, but the only way we can do so is by entering into an economy of exchange. We do give each other gifts all the time, but just as the possibility of painting a landscape is the impossibility of a perfect representation of that landscape, so too the very possibility of gift-giving is the impossibility of a *pure* unconditional gift as such:

> If the gift is annulled in the economic odyssey of the circle as soon as it appears *as* gift or as soon as it signifies *itself* as gift, there is no longer any "logic of the gift," and one may safely say that a consistent discourse on the gift becomes impossible: It misses its object and always speaks, finally of something else.   (GT: 24)

As soon as a pure gift is given it disappears leaving only a trace behind. We can never return or re-collect an unconditional gift.

What does it mean, therefore, to give an impossible gift? We can never simply step outside the circle of exchange. We are always inscribed in our traditional linguistic, cultural and political economies and, as Derrida reminds us, we have to "give economy its chance" (GT: 30). Derrida therefore tries to situate himself between what is possible and the impossible, between the conditional and the unconditional.[5] To desire the impossible gift, the gift without expectation of return, is a way of sensitizing ourselves to the fact that the identity of our traditions and institutions can never acquire absolute status, that they can always be reformed in the light of unforeseen appeals for justice. To have a passion for the impossible or the unconditional means that you desire what you know to be impossible – because of the claim that our conditional economies (language, tradition, etc.) make on you – so as to prevent the conditional from becoming *too* conditional. The desire that one day there will be no more poverty in the world is an impossible desire, but that is precisely why we desire it. In so doing we refuse to accept that there is nothing more we can do, and always push ourselves to do more. So when Derrida says that the pure gift is impossible, he is simply saying that because the gift by its very nature must be afforded unconditionally, and because I cannot actually grant the gift without wanting and desiring to do so, thereby drawing both myself and the other into a reciprocal economy, the gift is always already annulled. But it is precisely this impossibility of the gift that impassions me to push against the limits of our conditional economies in an attempt to open them up to the possibility of improvement.[6]

We can see how our two models of memory correspond to the two logics of the gift. Our traditional conceptions of identity and memory repeat the logic of circular economy. In the same way that a gift is given in the full knowledge that it will eventually be returned, memory presupposes an original presence, which is temporarily deferred, only to be recollected later. Memory, therefore, is the recovery of an original presence in a circular economy of exchange. Derrida, in contrast, wants to think memory in terms of the *unconditional* gift. As the catastrophe of memory testifies to the impossibility of recollection, so too the unconditional gift testifies to a "radical forgetting", which shatters all expectations of recollection and return. From the moment of its inscription in an economy of exchange, the pure gift disappears. And, as Derrida remarks, "The thought of this radical forgetting as thought of the gift should accord with a certain experience of the *trace* as *cinder* or *ashes* in the sense in which we have tried to approach it elsewhere" (GT: 17). Just as the cinders of memory testify to the work of mourning as the passion and desire to always do more, to strive to remember more, so too the unconditional gift inspires us to push against the constraints of our conditional laws and economies in an attempt to make them more open and hospitable towards the future.

Hegel and the Jews

Of course, Derrida was not the first thinker to highlight the importance of memory in understanding identity. From the Platonic discourse of *anamnesis*, the attempt to recall and remember the intelligible realm of the Forms, to Hegel's speculative project of *Aufhebung* and *Erinnerung* as recollection and remembrance, to Nietzsche's genealogy and Heidegger's thinking of gathering and repetition, the history of philosophy is a history of memory (P: 382). But for all their diversity and complexity, all of these interpretations have one thing in common. They all conceive of memory as the recollection or gathering of an originary presence. They all presuppose that at some future point in time, everything will eventually be recollected and accounted for. The paradigmatic example of memory as the recollection of presence is the speculative philosophy of Hegel. G. W. F. Hegel was a nineteenth-century thinker whose philosophy had a considerable influence on Derrida's work. While many of his deconstructive strategies have their roots in Hegel, Derrida's entire body of work can be understood as a searing critique of the totalizing logic, which dominates the Hegelian system. We shall compare and contrast Derrida to Hegel throughout this book, but for the moment it is important to understand how Hegel exemplifies a philosophy of memory and recollection in terms of the circular economy of the gift.

For Hegel, history is the dialectical unfolding of Spirit (*Geist*). Actual empirical history, the actual events of existing individuals, cultures, traditions and so on are but particular moments in the greater movement of Universal Spirit. According to Hegel, history moves towards a predetermined end or *telos*, when Spirit will literally re-collect (*Aufhebung*) itself, when all particulars will be consumed by, and accorded their proper place in, the all encompassing totalizing grasp of the universal.

Actual history is but the means by which Universal Spirit attempts to recover its lost origins: its identity as pure self-presence. For Hegel memory is absolute. Spirit remembers everything and everything is recollected. Everything that resists or cannot find its place within the totalizing grasp of the universal is either negated and interiorized (*Erinnerung*) or excluded. Spirit remembers and reappropriates only what is proper to itself, and everything that resists or does not fit is simply forgotten.

11

Hegel once wrote that "the whole of philosophy resembles a circle of circles" ([1830] 1991: §15), and his speculative system, like the conditional economy of the gift, is an exemplary example of a circular economy of exchange: beginning with a simple presence (Spirit), it temporarily goes out of itself, only to return to itself later. Spirit strives to mediate what is foreign to it with the aim of reducing this otherness to sameness, so as to become one with itself. Like someone who gives a gift as a means to receive something in return, Spirit seeks only "to constitute its own unity, and precisely, to get its own identity recognized so that identity comes back to it, so that it can reappropriate its identity: as its property" (GT: 10–11). Within Hegel's circular logic everything will eventually be recollected. There can be no room for resistance or particularity. All differences are interiorized and reduced to the order of the same.

One of the key differences between Hegel and Derrida is illustrated in terms of their respective attitudes to the figure of the Jew and the Jewish faith. Everything that resists recollection, all the blind spots, ghosts and ruins, and everything that fails to find its place in the universal truth of absolute knowledge is embodied, for Hegel, in the figure of the Jew. Whereas the Greek *logos* embodies truth, harmony and beauty, for Hegel the Jew embodies resistance and non-belonging. Like the cut of circumcision, the Jew is cut from his homeland, destined nomadically to roam the desert. He founds an abstract Law as a means to constitute himself as the "favorite slave of an infinite power": a God who forever remains distant and alien to him (G: 46a). For Hegel, the Jew is ugly, "lacking" the "spirit of beauty". He is cut in two, and the very tragedy of his cut is abominable. Derrida quotes Hegel:

> The great tragedy (*Trauerspiel*) of the Jewish people is no Greek tragedy; it can arouse neither terror nor pity, for both of these arise only out of the fate which follows from the inevitable slip of a beautiful being (*schönen Wesens*); it can arouse horror (*Abscheu*) alone. The fate of the Jewish people is the fate of Macbeth who stepped out of nature itself, clung to alien Beings, and so in their service had to trample and slay everything holy in human nature, had at last to be forsaken by his gods (since these were objects and he their slave) and be dashed to pieces on his faith itself.   (G: 40a)

Like Abraham, the Jew has to kill the thing he loves: "The Jew does not love beauty. Suffice it to say that, nothing else, he does not love" (G: 40a). The Jew has no place in the infinite crusade of Hegel's Greco-Christian economy. For Hegel, the task of philosophy is to exorcise the spectral figure of the Jew from the onward march of speculative recollection.

The figure of the Jew, however, plays a very different role in the work of Derrida. The traumatic experiences of anti-Semitism, as well as his own sense of unease within the traditional Jewish community, recur again and again throughout Derrida's work. Since his earlier work on Edmund Jabes and Emmanuel Levinas to the texts on the shibboleth and circumcision, Jewish themes have always been at the foreground of Derrida's writing.[7]

For Derrida the Jew embodies everything that resists or is excluded from Hegel's speculative economy. Whether the migrant worker, the political prisoner or the Jewish people themselves, the figure of the Jew represents all those who are exiled and do not belong. All Derrida's texts are distinctly marked by the Jewish figures of the cut and circumcision: "Circumcision, that's all I've ever talked about, consider the discourse on the limit, margins, marks, *marches* etc. ..." (C: 70). Like Hegel's circular economy, circumcision also follows the trajectory of a circle. But as the cut of circumcision for the Jew marks an alliance, an opening towards the other as "wholly other" (God), so too circumcision, like the unconditional gift, accounts for the cut or "disjointing link" of all circular economies; the cut that opens them up to everything that is excluded and on the outside: "Like a wound ... opened to the stranger, to the other, to the neighbor, to the guest, to whomever" (S: 56). If Hegel's philosophy is the attempt to restore and recover the familial heritage of the Greek *logos*, then for Derrida circumcision is the figure of all that is cut away from the purity of the origin and the authority of the patriarch.

Circumcision also accounts for a simultaneous belonging and non-belonging. It accounts both for inclusion and belonging to a determinate faith and community, while at the same time signing the mark of exclusion and non-belonging, of exile and persecution. Circumcision is a *partage* (partition, partaking) which in French "names difference, the line of demarcation or the parting of the waters, scission, caesura, as well as participation, that which is divided because it is shared or held in common, imparted and partaken of" (S: 31).

So *contra* Hegel, the figure of the Jew, like the unconditional gift, accounts for everything that shatters and resists the enclosure of speculative recollection. Whereas Hegel thinks memory in terms of an economy of exchange in which memories are exchanged like presents, Derrida thinks the catastrophe of memory in terms of the unconditional gift, which resists assimilation and enclosure within Hegel's all-embracing system. And, like circumcision, the work of mourning also accounts for the undecidability of life and death, for *both* belonging *and* non-belonging while reducible to *neither* one *nor* the other.

The work of mourning

What exactly do we do when we mourn? What does it mean to mourn someone or something? When a loved one dies our first instinct is to cling to them, to keep them close and hold fast to their memory. But we know that at the same time we have to let them go. As much as we desire to keep them with us and safeguard their presence, we can never do so. The loved one has departed. They are present no more.

In order to overcome the trauma of mourning we may be tempted to give in to one of two extremes. Either we may be tempted to absolutely let the other go, to just accept the fact that they are gone, forget that they ever existed and get on with our lives or, like the melancholic parent who, unable to accept the death of a child, maintains their bedroom exactly as they left it, we may attempt to carry on as if the loved one is still present, refusing to upset everyday rituals, personal belongings and so on.[8]

Contrary to these two extremes, which attempt to *either* keep the loved one *or* let them go, Derrida desires to do both, resisting the desire to reduce the work of mourning to either one or the other. Derrida desires *both* to keep the other *and* let them go: "We are left then with having to do and not do both at once, with having to correct one infidelity by the other" (WM: 45). We want to let the other go, we want to respect the fact that they have departed, but at the same time we want to keep them close, we want to keep them in our memory.

This is the experience of mourning that is familiar to anyone who has ever lost a loved one. Anyone who has ever experienced the trauma of mourning knows the impossibility of Hegel's injunction that we should simply accord the departed loved one their proper place and get on with our lives. Not only is this impossible, but we desire and affirm this impossibility. This is precisely what allows us to keep the loved one close, to remember the events of their life while allowing them, even though they have departed, a continuing presence and influence in our lives.

> Mourning is an interiorization of the dead other, but it is also the contrary. Hence the impossibility of completing one's mourning and even the will not to mourn are also forms of fidelity. ... I cannot complete my mourning for everything I lose, because I want to keep it, and at the same time, what I do best is to mourn, is to lose it, because by mourning, I keep it inside me. And it is this terrible logic of mourning that I talk about all the time, that I am concerned with all the time. (P: 152)

There are therefore two logics at work here, both of which follow a circular movement. Hegel's logic always starts with an originary presence, which is temporarily deferred, only to be recollected again later. The work of mourning also follows a circular movement, but for Derrida the circle never reaches completion. He desires *both* to keep the other *and* to let the other go while reducing the work of mourning to *neither* one *nor* the other. The impossibility of the circle ever coming to completion is what drives our desire to mourn: to resurrect the ghosts of the dead, the traces of all those who resist and survive the universalizing sweep of Hegel's speculative system. Like the figures of the impossible, the gift and the Jew, all of Derrida's many neologisms – *différance*, archi-writing, iterability and so on – are figures of mourning that attempt to articulate and realize this impossible desire.

As works of mourning, Derrida's texts are littered with the funeral remains of ashes and cinders, spectres and ruins: the "thought of incineration of the holocaust of cinders runs through all my texts".[9] Contrary to Hegel, for whom memory and mourning follow a circular trajectory with presence and recollection as their organizing centre, for Derrida, the centre is "failure" and incompletion: the centre is "under ashes ... the center is mourning" (WD: 297).

The cinder also testifies to the work of mourning as fire and burning. To burn something is to desire *both* to keep it *and* let it go. In *The Post Card*, a collection of postcards that Derrida writes to an anonymous lover, he advises "Keep what you burn, such is the demand. Mourn what I send you" (PC: 60). The only way to preserve and keep something safe is to burn it. Take the example of a love letter. The only way to safeguard its intimate secrecy, the only way to prevent it from falling into the public domain and the risk of exposure and interpretation, is to burn it. To keep it, one has to let it go, to set it to the flame, to "love by setting on fire" (MO: 50).

> It is a very great safeguard to learn by heart instead of writing ...
> It is impossible for what is written not to be disclosed ... Farewell
> and believe. Read this letter now at once many times and burn it – I
> hope this one won't get lost ... Reread this letter ... burn it. There
> are ashes there [*Il y a la cendre*]. (D: 170–71)

The figures of the sun and fire play a crucial role in the history of Western philosophy from Plato to Hegel and beyond. The sun is the source of pure light, the giver of heat and of life, the origin of presence and truth. But in order to consume and recollect itself, the sun has to burn and destroy. In order to keep, it has to let go. For Hegel, the circular movement of Spirit follows this heliocentric logic, burning all the particulars of empirical history in order finally to recollect and consummate itself in the pure light of absolute knowledge:

Pure and figureless, this light burns all. It burns itself in the all burn-ing [*le brûle-tout*] it is, leaves, of itself or anything, no trace, no mark, no sign of passage. Pure consuming destruction, pure effusion of light without shadow, noon without contrary, without resistance, without obstacle ..."   (G: 238–43a)

Everything is assimilated within the circular enclosure of Hegel's specula-tive reason. The Hegelian fire consumes all without remainder: "a great holocaustic fire, a burn everything into which we would throw finally, along with our entire memory, our names, the letters, photos, small objects, keys, fetishes etc." (PC: 40).

The work of mourning is neither absolute destruction (letting go) nor the pure light of an all-consuming sun (keeping). Whereas for Hegel memory burns and recollects everything, leaving no remains, resistance or obstacle, Derrida proposes that there are only ashes and cinders (*il y a la cendre*). Cin-ders disrupt and resist the all-burning logic of Hegel's speculative economy (ashes do not burn). These ashes resist our attempts to burn and safeguard everything. No matter how much we may want to preserve the intimacy of a love letter for example, even if we burn it there are still ashes there (*il y a là cendre*). Even the burnt cinders of a love letter lend themselves to the possibility of public exposure and interpretation.

When one thinks of the figure of the trace, one might think of a footprint in the snow, which testifies to the absence of a former determinate presence. But the cinder testifies to the "catastrophe of memory", the absolute impos-sibility of memory and recollection. If we were walking along a forest path and came across burning cinders, we can only assume that they testify to the former presence of something, but something absolutely indeterminate. It is impossible to resurrect or recollect a presence from cinders. But the fading and glowing heat of cinders testifies to the interminable desire of the work of mourning: "the incubation of the fire lurking beneath the dust" (CS: 59). While we know that we can never resurrect our loved ones, we still *desire,* in an act of love and fidelity, to do so: the work of mourning is love itself.

It is important to emphasize that the work of mourning is not a mere metaphor for Derrida: "All work in general works at mourning" (WM: 142). It is a focal point for conceptual and theoretical activity, one of the "organizing themes of the entire deconstructive critique that I am attempt-ing to make" (MS: 235):

For a long time now I myself have been "working" at mourning – if I can put it that way – or have been letting myself be worked by the question of mourning, by the aporias of the "work of mourn-ing", on the resources and the limits of psychoanalytic discourse on this subject, and on a certain coextensivity between work in general and the work of mourning. The work of mourning is not one work among others. All work involves this transformation, this appropriating idealization, this internalization that characterizes "mourning". (FWT: 78)

To mourn identity, to subject our traditional ideals, values and institutions to a work of mourning, is to desire both to keep and to let go, and to desire that this work never come to completion. In this way we can preserve the memory of the past while opening it up to the future. To do justice to our identities is to mourn them, to love by setting on fire, faithfully tending to the burning embers of the remains.

Conclusion

Derrida's entire philosophy is a work of memory and mourning. "I have only one project", Derrida remarked in an interview. "My first desire is not to produce a philosophical work or a work of art: it is to preserve memory" (P: 142–3). Derrida desires to preserve our traditional forms of identity and belonging. But whereas the philosophical tradition thinks identity and belonging in terms of presence and the possibility of fully recollecting the past, for Derrida our identities are never complete. No matter how much we desire to resurrect the past, the work of mourning testifies to this impossibility and the interminable demand that there is always more to be done: "What I dream of is not only the narration of a past that is inaccessible to me, but a narrative that would also be a future, that would determine a future" (P: 206–7). Derrida's entire philosophical project can be understood in terms of the interminable logic of this mourning-work. While we traditionally approach the question of identity in terms of presence, plenitude and recollection, for Derrida identity is always haunted by the spectral traces of absence, loss and death.

"Deconstruction is anachronism in synchronism", Derrida once commented in dialogue with Gianni Vattimo. "It is a matter of attuning to something that is out of joint and out of tune" (TS: 82). Contrary to the great systematic philosophers who think they can cheat absence, loss and death, gathering all of time and history into one all-embracing harmonious narrative, Derrida affirms the inescapability of death, attuning himself to the fundamental dis-adjustment of memory and mourning. In any given context, whether it is a philosophical text or a political or cultural institution, Derrida attempts to attune his reading to the "disjointing links", the blind spots and reserves of memory, that cut and resist all inclusion within the circle of adjustment and recollection.

Derrida does not want to do away with presence and identity or our traditional values and institutions. He desires these things more than anything else: "what I know my desire to be, in other words you: living speech, presence itself, proximity, the proper ..." (PC: 194). It is a popular misconception that deconstruction attempts to raze our values and institutions to the ground. But contrary to his reputation as an iconoclast hell bent on wanton destruction, Derrida desires to *keep* and maintain our traditional ideals and institutions: "I want to keep everything" (P: 152). Indeed, he often refers to himself as a "conservative person" (VR: 5) who believes "in the necessity for a certain tradition, in particular for political reasons that are nothing less than traditionalist" (TT: 42). The desire to belong, the deep longing to have an identity, a language and a tradition in which one can feel at home, is constant throughout Derrida's work.

Derrida argues, however, that in order to do justice to our most cherished ideals and values, we need to be ruthlessly critical of all those who complacently believe that they have fallen from the heavens. Our identities all have complex historical genealogies, and in order to comprehend them fully we need to engage in a detailed critical analysis of the historical context from which they emerged. But while our attempts to comprehend fully our historical past will always be incomplete, it is precisely this impossibility that impassions our desire to mourn the past and do it justice:

> It is necessary first of all to know and to know how to reaffirm what comes "before us," which we therefore receive even before choosing ... it is necessary to do everything to appropriate a past even though we know that it remains fundamentally inappropriable, whether it is a question of philosophical memory or the precedence of a language, a culture and filiation in general. What does it mean to reaffirm? It means not simply accepting this heritage but relaunching it otherwise and keeping it alive.   (FWT: 3)

Derrida desires to subject our values and institutions to a radical critique, but what distinguishes him from so many of his contemporaries is that he only deconstructs and critiques that which he loves. Derrida is not interested in simply accusing the Western tradition of all manner of abuse and oppression. He wants to preserve our intellectual traditions but argues that we can only do so by opening them up – especially when they prove resistant – to the risks of the future and what is "to come".

When it comes to our traditional forms of identity and belonging, therefore, Derrida desires both to keep and let go, which is why he describes himself as a "faithful perjurer" (PC: 198), who approaches the tradition like one who "caresses with claws" (MO: 66). But while Derrida applies his critical skills to our traditional forms of identity and belonging, he always does so in an attitude of "scrupulous fidelity", desiring to preserve memory while giving it a future: "I feel best when my sense of emancipation preserves the memory of what it emancipates from" (TS: 43).

Throughout this book we shall see Derrida apply the logic of mourning to some of the classical themes and questions in the history of philosophy. Whether it is a question of speech and writing, presence and absence, or identity and difference, Derrida always subjects the identities of these economies to the both/and neither/nor logic of the work of mourning. All of Derrida's neologisms and deconstructive strategies repeat this logic, denoting the irretrievable loss that gives rise to mourning. That is why Derrida's texts are haunted by the impossible figures of ghosts and tombs, spectres and monsters. All economies that attempt to organize themselves around presence, completeness and life cannot – despite all their attempts and protestations to the contrary – completely exorcise the ghosts of absence and loss, incompleteness and death. In the midst of life we are always in death. The work of mourning is Derrida's attempt to account for this impossible relation.

CHAPTER TWO

Death and *différance*: philosophy and language

Derrida is primarily a philosopher of language. He devoted his entire career to demonstrating how all of our experience is mediated by language, writing and textuality. We can never have access to any kind of experience that would not already be structured by language. The only way we can comprehend anything at all is if we can conceptualize it to some degree. But what does this have to do with memory? Historical memory, the desire to recollect and preserve the past, is only possible by means of texts and documents, monuments and archives, all of which are forms of what Derrida means by *writing*. If there were no writing, there would be no history and no possibility of memory. But writing is always partial and incomplete; it is composed of multifarious marks and traces, and can always function in the absence of an original event or "presence". It is precisely because memory is inseparable from writing that memory itself is fragmentary and incomplete.

Derrida is critical of the philosophical tradition that attempts to efface the necessity of writing from identity and historical memory. This tradition always attempts to think identity in terms of a *teleology* of memory. By teleology, Derrida means the attempt to recover and recollect a determinate end (*telos*). This "end" is the conviction that eventually everything can be recollected, that the past can be gathered into a harmonious whole. But Derrida argues that our attempts to recollect the past are always structured by language and writing, absence and loss; the *telos* of full recollection is destined to fail. In this chapter we shall examine some of the key figures of mourning – archi-writing, dissemination, *différance* and iterability – that Derrida employs to account for the irreducibility of writing within all experience, identity and memory.

Speech and writing

Derrida's work is one long attempt to show how loss and death haunt everything, but most especially the writings of those thinkers who believe they can cheat death. If Hegel is one such thinker, Plato is another, which is why Derrida devotes one of his earliest works to a deconstructive account of Plato's *Phaedrus*. In his essay "Plato's Pharmacy" (D: 61–171), Derrida shows how the undecidability of life and death, of presence and absence, plays itself out in terms of speech and writing. Towards the end of the dialogue, Socrates (Plato's teacher) and Phaedrus (a young Athenian) argue the merits of speech and writing. Socrates, like Plato, argues for the superiority of speech over the dead repetition of writing. When something is written down it exposes itself to the risk of being misinterpreted and abused in the hands of people who are unqualified to comprehend its true meaning. In speech, on the other hand, the speaker is present to accompany and guarantee the true meaning of the communication. For Plato and Socrates, speech is the medium of identity, completion and adjustment; writing is the medium of difference, incompletion and dis-adjustment.

In the *Phaedrus*, Socrates recounts the ancient story of Theuth, an Egyptian divinity who is credited with inventing numbers and calculation, geometry and astronomy, draughts and dice, and above all writing (*grammata*). Socrates narrates how Theuth presented his inventions to Thamus, the king of all Egyptians, arguing for the usefulness of each one. When it came to writing, Theuth says, "This discipline, my King, will make the Egyptians wiser and will improve their memories: my invention is a recipe (*pharmakon*) for both memory and wisdom" (274c–e).

In response, Thamus argues that writing will have the exact opposite effect that Theuth intends. Those who write will stop exercising their memory and will become forgetful, relying on the external material marks of writing instead of their own internal capacity to remember things. As for wisdom, writing offers only the semblance of true learning. Without the presence of proper instruction anyone can pick up a written text and feign the appearance of wisdom (274e–275b).

Like Thamus, Socrates (who never wrote anything) argues that genuine knowledge and education can only happen through living memory and speech. When a student is in the presence of a teacher, for example, the teacher can guarantee the communication of their intended meaning through the medium of the voice. In this scenario, the teacher knows exactly what they mean to say and whether or not the student has understood. The student then has the capacity to recall this originary presence – living memory – rather than having to rely on the external and lifeless marks of writing.

That is why, for Plato and Socrates, writing is an evil. As soon as something is written down it is divorced from the animating intention that gives it life and guarantees its proper meaning. Genuine meaning always communicates through the medium of the voice: a living presence, which accompanies what it means to say. Writing, on the other hand, is a "dead repetition" (D: 135), lifeless and errant: "an outlaw, a pervert, a bad seed, a vagrant, an adventurer, a bum" (D: 148). Unable to answer for itself, it is subjected to the vicissitudes and arbitrary whims of whoever encounters it. If the voice is the animating breath of a living presence, then writing is the foul stench of errancy and death. This privileging of speech over writing is what Derrida calls "phonocentrism":

> When I speak, not only am I conscious of being present for what I think, but I am conscious also of keeping as close as possible to my thought, or to the "concept," a signifier that does not fall into the world, a signifier that I hear as soon as I emit it, that seems to depend upon my pure and free spontaneity, requiring the use of no instrument, no accessory, no force taken from the world. Not only do the signifier and the signified seem to unite, but also, in this confusion, the signifier seems to erase itself or to become transparent, in order to allow the concept to present itself as what it is, referring to nothing other than its presence. (Pos: 22)

"Memory and truth cannot be separated", for Plato (D: 105). Living memory (*mneme*) is the unveiling of truth (*alētheia*) in its self-presentation to itself. Memory as writing (*hypomnesis*) on the other hand, conceals and buries the truth (*lethe*), "simultaneously increas[ing] the domains of death, of nontruth, of nonknowledge" (D: 105). At best, writing is just a reminder; at worst, it is a poison. Writing always increases the risk that one may become dependent on lifeless signs rather than the living presence of internal memory: "the substitution of the mnemonic device for live memory, of the prosthesis for the organ substituting the passive, mechanical 'by heart' for the active reanimation of knowledge, for its reproduction in the present" (D: 108).

According to Derrida, however, Plato cannot maintain this rigorous distinction between speech and writing. The alleged pure presence of speech and living memory already contains within itself the traces of difference and absence, dis-adjustment and death: precisely the sinister qualities that Plato wants to assign to writing.[1] But Plato himself is aware of the contamination of memory (*mneme*) by absence and loss (*hypomnesis*), when he concedes that living memory is finite, and therefore contains within itself the inevitability of its own death.

> The evil slips in within the relation of memory to itself, in the general organization of the mnesic activity. Memory is finite by nature. Plato recognizes this in attributing life to it. As in the case of all living organisms, he assigns it, as we have seen, certain limits. A limitless memory would in any event be not memory but infinite self-presence. Memory always therefore already needs signs in order to recall the non-present, with which it is necessarily in relation. The movement of dialectics bears witness to this. Memory is thus contaminated by its first substitute: *hypomnesis*.   (D: 109)

Speech and memory are always contaminated by writing. This contamination is an example of what Derrida calls "the logic of supplementarity". We normally think of a supplement as something that is added to something else that is already complete. This is how Plato views the relationship between speech and writing. But for Derrida the supplement is not a secondary prosthesis that is added to identity; rather, it is already *within* identity. We see this logic at work in Plato's text where Plato himself admits that speech already has holes in it. Speech *requires* writing in order to be what it is. So Plato's attempt to maintain a strict inside–outside distinction, to banish writing from the pure interiority of speech and living memory, is structurally impossible: "The outside is already within the work of memory" (D: 109).

Of course Derrida is not suggesting that writing, understood as written marks on a page, is somehow prior or interior to speech. Again, what Derrida means by writing – what he terms *archi-writing* – is the qualities that are normally attributed exclusively to writing: difference, deferral, repetition and death. Derrida's point is that these *same* qualities are already within speech and living memory. Plato cannot recollect the plenitude of speech because presence is already marked by absence, loss and death. Despite his efforts to set up a qualitative distinction between the purity of speech on the one hand, and the errancy of writing on the other, Plato's own text undermines his ability to maintain this distinction. The speech–writing opposition is undecidable: the two terms bleed into and supplement one another. And this undecidability marks a cut in the circular movement of Plato's economy. The very possibility of the speech–writing opposition is the *impossibility* of maintaining this opposition.

Derrida illustrates this undecidability in the figure of the *pharmakon*: a Greek word that means both "remedy" and "poison", and which was used by Theuth to describe the merits of writing. Plato attempts to resolve this undecidability by resolutely translating it as "poison". As *pharmakon*, writing is not a remedy; it is a poison and must be banished.

Derrida notes the etymological bond between the term *pharmakon* and the Greek word *pharmakos*, which means, "scapegoat". In ancient Greek culture there was a festival called the Thargelia, on the sixth day of which the Athenians purified the city. The ritual involved projecting the evil of society on to a scapegoat, who was then expelled from the city taking the evil with him:

> The city's body proper thus reconstitutes its unity, closes around the security of its inner courts ... by violently excluding from its territory the representative of an external threat or aggression. That representative represents the otherness of evil that comes to affect or infect the inside by unpredictably breaking into it.   (D: 133)[2]

The city attempts to gather and enclose itself in the figure of a circle, banishing to the outside everything it is not. But, as Derrida notes, the *pharmakos* was always already inside the city walls, and played an important part in constituting its identity:

> Yet the representative of the outside [*pharmakos*] is nonetheless constituted, regularly granted its place by the community, chosen, kept, fed, etc., in the very heart of the inside. These parasites were as a matter of course domesticated by the living organism that housed them at its expense. The Athenians regularly maintained a number of degraded and useless beings at the public expense; and when any calamity, such as plague, drought, or famine, befell the city, they sacrificed two of these outcasts as scapegoats.   (D: 133)

Like the *pharmakos*, the *pharmakon* also accounts for the undecidability of the inside and the outside, remedy and poison, speech and writing:

> If the *pharmakon* is "ambivalent," it is because it constitutes the medium in which opposites are opposed, the movement and the play that links them among themselves, reverses them or makes one side cross over into the other (soul/body, good/evil, inside/outside, memory/forgetfulness, speech/writing, etc.).   (D: 127)

Plato attempts to banish writing as *pharmakon* from the enclosure of speech and living memory. But like the *pharmakos*, writing is already inside speech. As a figure of mourning the *pharmakon* accounts for the possibility of *both* speech *and* writing, while reducible to *neither* one *nor* the other: "the *pharmakon* is neither remedy nor poison, neither good nor evil, neither the inside nor the outside, neither speech nor writing ... Neither/nor, that is simultaneously either/or" (Pos: 42–3). The undecidability of the *pharmakon* haunts and disturbs the economy of Plato's text: "[it] cannot be simply assigned a site within what it situates, [it] cannot be subsumed under concepts whose contours it draws, [it] leaves only its ghost to a logic that can only seek to govern it insofar as logic arises from it" (D: 103). Despite his best efforts, Plato cannot exorcise the ghost of the *pharmakon*. It resists all his attempts to settle speech and writing into a rigorous opposition.

In the *Phaedrus*, therefore, we have a classic example of an attempt to construct a closed circular economy around a teleology of complete and total recollection. Plato sets up a circular movement whereby speech passes through writing as a means to recollect itself in the pure presence of living memory. But, as Derrida demonstrates, writing is already inside speech and shatters its illusions of purity and plenitude. Derrida illustrates the impossibility of this teleology by attuning his reading to the *pharmakon*, the spectral undecidability of which marks a cut in the circular economy of Plato's text. The *pharmakon* resists Plato's attempts to fix and stabilize its meaning. But for Derrida it is precisely this impossibility of domesticating the undecidability of the *pharmakon* that makes it possible to read Plato's text anew and give it fresh life. And this possibility is what Derrida means by "dissemination".

Dissemination

The term "dissemination" accounts for the structural undecidability at work within any meaningful text. Like a scattering of seeds (*seme*), it accounts for the fact that a given text can always produce a plurality of readings. Dissemination challenges the traditional model of the book that presupposes a single unifying interpretation, which can be reduced to the animating intention of its author. According to this view, the task of reading and interpretation is merely to recollect the *telos* of this original intention. But, as we have just seen in Derrida's reading of the *Phaedrus*, the possibility of different interpretations is always contained within the text itself. To help us to understand what Derrida means by this let us turn to the efforts of an earlier thinker who also challenges the systematic attempt to enclose the meaning of a text within a single determinate interpretation.

Søren Kierkegaard, a philosopher who had a considerable influence on Derrida, went to extreme lengths to rescue writing from the systematic procedure of what he called bookbinding: the attempt to force a single dogmatic interpretation on a text.[3] Bookbinding for Kierkegaard, like Derrida, is the frantic attempt by those who wish to preserve the totality of a closed economy: to keep the disseminative play in check.

In *Stages on Life's Way* (1980), Kierkegaard gives a response to all those who would attempt to enforce this closed economy. In the apt name of his pseudonym, Hilarius Bookbinder, Kierkegaard writes for the amusement of the reader a "truthful history of the book" (1980: 3). In this little fragment, the pseudonym reports that "several years ago" a Mr Literatus left some manuscripts with Hilarius for the purpose of having them bound. Being in no hurry, Mr Literatus imposed no time restrictions on the bookbinder, and the manuscripts remained in the latter's possession for more than three months, during which time Mr Literatus died, "and his heirs, who were abroad, received the books through the probate court" (*ibid.*). Believing the matter closed, having been reimbursed for his labour, Hilarius suddenly came upon "a small package of handwritten papers", which, after some speculation, both he and his wife were forced to conclude belonged to the late Mr Literatus. As so much time had elapsed, and because no one had laid claim to the papers, the bookbinder "stitched them together in a colored paper folder so that they would not lie around and clutter up the shop" (*ibid.*: 4). However, the bookbinder did utilize the "book" every so often: he used it to educate his children in the art of reading aloud, and encouraged them to copy pages from it so as to imitate "the beautiful letters and flourishes" in the art of "penmanship".

Shortly thereafter, a "normal-school graduate and candidate in philosophy" became teacher to one of the bookbinder's sons. On seeing the stitched-up papers, he asked to borrow the "book". Hilarius offered to make him a present of it, "but he was too honorable ... so he borrowed it". After returning the writings to the bookbinder, the tutor exclaimed: "You presumably were unaware of what a glorious gift and donation providence has allotted to your household in this book you so casually wanted to give away. If it comes into the right hands, a book such as this is worth its weight in gold" (*ibid.*: 5). Hilarius concludes his history of the book with the following reflection:

> So it had come to pass as the good normal-school graduate and candidate in philosophy advised me ... that my service was greater because it was not one book I would publish but several books, probably by several authors. In other words, my learned friend assumes that here must have been a fraternity, a society, or an association of which that Literatus had been the head or president and therefore had preserved the papers. (*Ibid.*: 6)

Kierkegaard's point is that after receiving the papers of Mr Literatus for a second time, the bookbinder has to assume that there is more than one voice speaking through the pages of the text, that they amount not only to one book, but many books by several authors. Derrida follows Kierkegaard in attempting to liberate the reading of a text from those who attempt to circumscribe it within a binding and the claim by any one author that, by appending their signature to a text, he or she has control over the destiny of the text: that no textual "play" or reinterpretation of the text's content is permissible. Any attempt to still the textual forces at play – Plato's attempt to check the undecidability of the *pharmakon* for example – signifies a denial by the author, or the bookbinder, of the fact that all books contain within themselves a certain structural undecidability and the possibility of being reinterpreted.

While the *telos* of a traditional reading is the attempt to organize a text around a single determinate reading, dissemination testifies to the fact that a reading is always partial and incomplete; there is always a possibility of multiple interpretations. The identity of any text – like *all* identity – is always marked by absence and loss, difference and deferral. Derrida uses the term *différance* to account for this structural differing and deferral and, like all Derrida's neologisms, *différance* is a little monstrous and maintains close ties with the impossible and death.

Différance

In Hebrew folklore we encounter a similar figure of mourning in the shape of the golem. A precursor of the alchemist's "homunculus" (a human figure made from base matter) and the various Frankenstein creatures of folk culture, the golem was a quasi-animate man-made creature: an attempt by man to imitate the act of divine creation. One such golem was the infamous Golem of Prague.

In 1580, so the legend goes, a rumour began to spread that a priest called Taddeush was about to accuse the Jews of Prague of a blood libel: the anti-Semitic charge that the blood of a Christian child was used in the Passover seder. Fearing the inevitable retribution that would befall the Jewish population of the city, Rabbi Loew ben Bezalel decided to create a golem to protect them. The attempt to create life, however, was strictly forbidden by Jewish law. It was seen as a form of idolatry and as the attempt to usurp God as the sole power capable of bestowing life. Using ancient Kabbalistic formulas, however, Rabbi Loew managed to interpret the text of the Hebrew Book of Creation (*Sefer Yetsirah*) – a text that was thought to contain the secret letter combination that God used when he created man – and successfully gave life to a creature he moulded from the clay of the banks of the Vltava river.

The golem protected the Jewish community and performed all kinds of useful tasks for the rabbi. On the eve of one particular Sabbath however, the golem ran amok and wreaked havoc on the streets of Prague. As part of the Kabbalistic ritual, Rabbi Loew had carved the word "*emeth*" meaning "truth" on the golem's forehead. When he eventually caught up with the golem he erased the first letter aleph from "*emeth*", leaving the word "*meth*" meaning "death", and at once the golem crumbled into ashes.

As a figure of mourning, the golem testifies to the impossible desire for pure presence, the desire to be God (pure presence as immortality, as the attempt to escape history, finitude and death). The lesson of the golem is that the pretension to have achieved the gift of bestowing life can only result in destruction and loss. The heart of life and truth ("emeth") conceals ashes, cinders and death ("meth").

Like all monsters, the golem is an undecidable figure that disturbs the comfort and security of our desires and beliefs. Both dead and alive, human and inhuman, monsters always threaten the security of our closed economies. Rather than confronting us from the "outside", the monster, like the *pharmakon*, always shows (*monstrare*) us a disturbance or undecidability that already resides on the "inside".

> A monster is a species for which we do not yet have a name, which does not mean that the species is abnormal, namely, the composition or hybridization of already known species. Simply, it *shows* itself [*elle se* montre] – that is what the word monster means – it shows itself in something that is not yet shown and that therefore looks like a hallucination, it strikes the eye, it frightens precisely because no anticipation had prepared one to identify this figure.   (P: 386)

The German word for "monstrous" is "*unheimlich*", which literally means "un-homely": that which disturbs the comfort and security of the home (*oikos*). All of Derrida's neologisms, his figures of mourning, are monstrous:

> I employ these words, I admit, … with a glance toward those who, in a society from which I do not exclude myself, turn their eyes away when faced by the as yet unnameable which is proclaiming itself and which can do so, as is necessary whenever a birth is in the offing, only under the species of the nonspecies, in the formless, mute, infant, and terrifying form of monstrosity.   (WD: 293)

Like the golem, *différance* is a "discursive monster" (P: 386) that attempts to disturb the security of the home (*oikos*); and just as the golem testifies to the impossibility of the desire for immortality, so too *différance* testifies to the impossibility of the desire for complete and full recollection.

The term *différance* is also particularly useful for Derrida as it contains a number of different meanings.[4] First of all it means difference in the usual sense of "French is different from English". It also means the French verb *différer*, which means both to differ and to defer. *Différance* also contains within it the present participle *différant*, which means the condition of differing or of deferring (as in "the differing opinions" or "the deferring decision"). Finally, *différance* accounts for the *activity* of differing and deferring.

Différance has a further strategic advantage by virtue of how it is spelled: the "a" is silent; it cannot be heard. When spoken, the words *différence* and *différance* sound exactly the same. So the "a" of *différance* accounts for everything that resists the Western privilege of phonocentrism: the authority of the animating presence of the spoken voice. Like the word "emeth" inscribed on the golem's forehead, *différance* only has force when it is written. And as the letter "aleph" marks the difference between life and death for the golem, so too the "a" of *différance* accounts for an economy of life and death for Derrida:[5]

> It is offered by a mute mark, by a tacit monument, I would even say by a pyramid, thinking not only of the form of the letter when it is printed as a capital, but also of the text in Hegel's *Encyclopedia* in which the body of the sign is compared to the Egyptian Pyramid. The *a* of *différance*, thus, is not heard; it remains silent, secret and discreet as a tomb: *oikesis*. And thereby let us anticipate the delineation of a site, the familiar residence and tomb of the proper in which is produced, by *différance*, the *economy of death*. (M: 4)

For Hegel, like Plato, written language or the sign is that which preserves for memory the original intuition of what has become alien to consciousness. The sign is a pyramid, a figure of the physical and the spiritual, presence and absence, life and death. The sign signifies death (the original intuition is no longer full) and life (it contains the spirit of the original intuition). But according to Hegel, consciousness can literally retrieve and resurrect the original intuition by negating the physicality of the material sign and interiorizing the spirit of all that is contained within it. So when we read "We hold these truths to be self-evident", for example, our consciousness can negate the physical materiality of these words and interiorize the original animating intention of Thomas Jefferson, which, according to Hegel, literally resides within the physical sign awaiting reanimation.[6]

Différance is also inhabited by a pyramid and a tomb in the figure of its capitalized "A". But for Derrida the sign is not a mere means to an end: the resurrection of an original presence. The materiality of the sign resists Hegel's attempts to assign it its proper place in his speculative economy, and continues to haunt and frustrate his pretensions to complete and total recollection. The pyramidical structure of *différance* accounts for the fact that we can never exorcise the traces of the dead. Just as the cinder resists the fires of Hegel's all-burning logic, so too the sign stands alone, like a pyramid in the desert sun, calling us to mourning and the risks of interpretation.

As a figure of mourning, then, *différance* accounts for the fact that while we do desire to resurrect the dead and bring them back to life, this desire is doomed to failure. And just as the erasure of the aleph from the Golem's forehead causes him to collapse into a pile of ashes, so too the "a" of *différance* accounts for the cinders and ashes of memory: the fact that memory and identity are always incomplete.

Différance also accounts for a *spatial* differing and *temporal* deferral at the heart of memory and identity. But what does it mean to say that identity is an effect of differing and deferral? We shall examine what Derrida means by temporal deferral below, but in order to understand what he means by spatial differing, we need to first examine the influence of Ferdinand de Saussure.

Structuralism

The term "structuralism" refers to a method of analysis that had considerable influence in a wide variety of intellectual disciplines in the twentieth century. The structuralist method played a decisive role in French intellectual life in particular, influencing the works of Claude Lévi-Strauss, Roland Barthes, Louis Althusser, Jacques Lacan and Michel Foucault, among others.[7]

Structuralism aims to explain particular events or units of meaning in terms of underlying structural laws. According to this methodology, individual units of meaning are not to be understood as self-enclosed identities, but according to their interrelationship within the totality of structural laws that determine them.

Lévi-Strauss for example, applies the structuralist method to anthropology. He argues that despite the appearance of irreconcilable differences between different cultures and societies, the structuralist method reveals that these societies all share certain mythic, symbolic and kinship structures. If we want to understand the difference between Western European society and that of Native North Americans for example, we need to understand their interrelationship in the context of these structural laws.

The founding father of structuralism is the Swiss linguist Ferdinand de Saussure (1857–1913). In his *Course in General Linguistics* (1959),[8] Saussure attempts to explain linguistics (the study of languages) in terms of a general "semiology". Saussure wants to move beyond the limitations of nineteenth-century linguistics – which concentrated on grammar, philology and the historical development of languages – by reconceiving linguistics in terms of a general science (*logos*) of signs (*semeia*).

Saussure challenges the traditional model of understanding language in terms of what language is *about*: what it corresponds to, or refers to, in the world. He analyses language as a self-regulating system. The meanings of words, signs and so on are determined by the internal structures of language as a whole, rather than their individual references to things in the world. Language is to be understood as a formal system of relations rather than individual instances of correspondence or reference to things.

In attempting to do this, he makes the distinction between language (*langue*) and speech (*parole*). *Parole* is any particular act of language, whereas *langue* is the systematic totality of all possible linguistic usage, which makes these individual acts possible. If we want to understand how language works as a whole, we need to engage in a detailed analysis of the structural laws of *langue* that determine all linguistic usage.

What an individual word actually refers to is completely arbitrary. Take the word "cat", for example. The relationship between this particular word and the actual animal in the world is merely an arbitrary custom of the English-speaking world. There is no essential relationship between the word "cat" and the thing to which it refers. If aliens landed from another planet they could analyse the word "cat" for a million years, but they would never be able to derive from it the actual animal to which we refer when we use this word. Saussure's point is that if we want to understand how language works we will not be able to do so by simply asking what language is about. All this can tell us is how we use language (in English we say "cat", in German we say "Katze") rather than how language itself works. So how does language work? How does the word "cat" derive its meaning?

All units of meaning are "signs", which function in the absence of the object, or "referent", which they represent. So the word "cat" allows us to speak of cats in the absence of an actual cat. As the relationship between the sign and its referent is purely arbitrary, in order to understand how language works Saussure turns to the composition of the sign itself.

The sign is composed of a signifier and a signified. The signifier is the material side of the sign. It can be graphic, such as the markings on this page, or phonic, such as the material sound waves of the human voice. The signified, on the other hand, is the concept or idea of the sign. So with the example "cat", the signifier is the material marks we have just typed, and the signified is the concept "cat" to which it refers (the actual animal is the "referent"). Now the distinction between signifier and signified is nothing new. Traditionally philosophers have always distinguished between the sensible and intelligible elements of language. Plato and Hegel, for example, distinguish between the idea (intelligible) and its material representation (sensible). The idea is the primary essence of meaning, while its sensible representation is always a secondary addition.

Saussure challenges this traditional view in two ways. First, he argues that the signifier and the signified are indissolubly related. You cannot separate the one from the other. A signified requires a material signifier in order to be articulated, and a signifier can only have a meaning by virtue of the signified we can recognize across its various material manifestations (for example if three different people write the word "cat", each of these signifiers will be different due to differences in handwriting, and so on, but we still recognize the same idea/signified "cat" common to all three, despite these material differences). The signifier and signified, therefore, are like the two sides, *recto* and *verso*, of a piece of paper.

Saussure's most radical innovation, however, is his claim that meaning is constituted in a system of differences. Language does not comprise atomic unities, each of which has its own meaning. The meaning of a word or sign is determined according to its difference from other words or signs within the system of language as a whole. This means that identities are an *effect* of differential relations. To get a better idea of what he means, imagine a blind person who acquires the power of sight. At first the world appears as a chaotic mix of sensual impressions. It is only by making distinctions and determining differences that they learn to identify the identity of individual things. They can only identify the meaning "cat", for example, in relation to "not-dog", "not-table", "not-car" and so on.

Similarly, a word or a sign only has a meaning by virtue of its difference from every other sign. We can only identify the word "cat" by virtue of its difference from the words "bat", "rat", "mat" and so on. "Cat" differs from "bat" on account of the difference between "c" and "b". But "c" can only have a meaning by virtue of its difference from "b" and every other sign. Every sign, therefore, contains within it the trace of every other sign within the system of language. No signifier has a complete identity or meaning. It always contains within it the traces of its differential relationships to every other signifier. Like the blind person above, we can only determine identities as an effect of these differences. And this applies to both the signifier and the signified as two sides of the same sheet of paper. Saussure writes:

> The conceptual side of value is made up solely of relations and differences with respect to the other terms of language, and the same can be said of its material side ... Everything that has been said up to this point boils down to this: in language there are only differences. Even more important: a difference generally implies positive terms between which the difference is set up; but in language there are only differences *without positive terms*. Whether we take the signified or the signifier, language has neither ideas nor sounds that existed before the linguistic system, but only conceptual and phonic

differences that have issued from the system. The idea or phonic substance that a sign contains is of less importance than the other signs that surround it.

(Saussure 1959: 117–18, 120; quoted in M: 10–11)

Saussure's influence is considerable. First, he problematizes the distinction and hierarchy between the sensible and the intelligible (which is just another version of the presence–absence, life–death distinction) and, secondly, he argues that the identity of any unit of meaning is an effect of differential relations.

By making linguistics (with its emphasis on spoken language), a division of a general semiology (which emphasizes the formal and differential characteristics of signs), Saussure greatly contributes to the overturning of the teleology of memory. Saussure testifies to the *catastrophe* of memory as the impossibility of any unit of identity recollecting itself in the form of a pure presence. All identities are marked by the traces of other elements in the signifying chain: presence is always inhabited by traces of absence.

Having affirmed this irreducible dis-adjustment at the heart of all identity, however, Saussure then *reinstates* a teleology of memory by privileging the "natural link" between thought and the voice and "everything that links the sign to *phone*" (Pos: 21). He makes the phonetic sign – which always presents itself in the immediacy and transparency of the spoken voice (*phone*) – the "pattern" for all signs in general. In so doing, Saussure falls back into the logic of phonocentrism, which undermines all the critical work he has undertaken.

According to Derrida, it was Saussure's continued reliance on the terms "sign", "signifier" and "signified" that inevitably led to the re-inscription of his general semiology in a metaphysics and teleology of the voice.[8] Derrida argues that the distinction between the signifier and the signified "inevitably leaves open the possibility of thinking a concept signified in and of itself, a concept simply present for thought, independent of a relationship to language, that is of a relationship to a system of signifiers" (Pos: 19). In order to avoid this trap, Derrida replaces the term "sign" with that of the "trace". If the sign runs the risk of effacing itself in the pure presence of the voice, the trace always testifies to the irreducibility of absence and loss. As we saw in Chapter 1, we never recollect a pure presence at the origin; there are only the traces of differences. So the meaning of any word is not determined by its own "internal essence" or identity; its meaning is always the effect of a differential play of traces.

The play of differences supposes, in effect, syntheses and referrals that forbid at any moment, or in any sense, that a simple element be *present* in and of itself, referring only to itself. Whether in the order of spoken or written discourse, no element can function as a sign without reference to another element which itself is not simply present. This interweaving results in each "element" – phoneme or grapheme – being constituted on the basis of the trace within it of the other elements of the chain or system ... There are only every-where, differences and traces of traces. (Pos: 26)

The identity of an element of language is never simply given. As Derrida remarks in *Positions*, "each allegedly 'simple term' is marked by the trace of another term, the presumed interiority of meaning is already worked upon by its own exteriority" (Pos: 33). Just as writing is always inside speech and living memory, so too the traces of differential relations are always inside identity. Identity is always marked by this relation to an outside. And this is what Derrida means by "spacing":

> [D]*ifférance*, then, is a structure and a movement no longer conceiv-able on the basis of the opposition presence/absence. *Différance* is the systematic play of differences, of the traces of differences, of the *spacing* by means of which elements are related to each other.
> (Pos: 27)

This structural "spacing" is not something that is added to self-identical elements after the fact. It is already contained within identity as the very condition of its possibility. If this were not the case – if a letter, a word or a sentence *could* gather itself into a single univocal meaning free of any rela-tion to an outside and difference – then its meaning would be exhausted in a "unique" utterance and we would not be able to cite it in different contexts.

Following Saussure, *différance* accounts for this spatial differing at the heart of all identity and meaning. In order to understand how *différance* also accounts for a temporal deferral, we need to turn to Derrida's seminal essay "Signature Event Context".[10]

Intentionality, absence and repetition

In "Signature Event Context", Derrida examines how the teleology of mem-ory understands the themes of intentionality, communication and context. According to this view, an author communicates his or her intentions in the form of oral or written marks to a determinate receiver. The *telos* of this circular economy is the resurrection of the original animating presence of the author from within the text. So when we read Plato's *Phaedrus*, for example, our objective (*telos*) is simply to reawaken the meaning of his original intention. Derrida intends to argue that not only can we *never* recollect the original intention of an author, but it is precisely the impossibility of doing so that makes possible all forms of meaningful communication in the first place. We have just seen how Derrida uses Saussure to argue that there are always traces of spatial difference within identity. In "Signature Event Context" Derrida uses the term "iterability" to account for the temporal deferral and possibility of repetition at the heart of all meaningful experience.

All forms of communication are determined by their context. Take the statement "Break a leg!" Its meaning when uttered in a drama theatre would be very different to its meaning when uttered during the course of an ill-tempered football match. According to the classical conception of communication, however, the possibility of potential misunderstanding can be avoided by paying attention to the determinate context in which the statement is uttered. In the context of a performance of *Hamlet*, for example, we can rest assured that Gertrude will not break Polonius's legs. But Derrida wants to challenge this sense of assurance and certainty. As we have seen, no context is ever absolutely determinable; it is always subject to dissemination and the possibility of multiple interpretations. There *are* contexts, however: meaning is always determined according to a determinate context. But Derrida's point is that this meaning can never be guaranteed. There is always the possibility that Polonius will have to keep an eye on Gertrude.

As in "Plato's Pharmacy", Derrida intends to challenge the classical conception of context and communication by "displacing a certain concept of writing" (M: 310). In order to illustrate the traditional conception of the relationship between communication and writing, Derrida turns to Etienne Condillac's *Essay on the Origin of Human Knowledge* (1973). Derrida chooses Condillac's work not only because of its explicit reflection on the origin and function of writing, but for the fact that it places writing under the authority of the category of communication. According to Condillac, already capable of communicating their thoughts and ideas to one another, men invented writing to perpetuate their ideas and "make them *known* to *absent* persons" (Condillac 1973: ch. 13, pt 2, §13; quoted in M: 312, Derrida's emphasis).

Following Plato and Hegel, Condillac argues that writing exists as a mere means to resurrect the intentions of an original author. People use writing to transmit and transport their intentions to others who are absent. In the absence of a determinate reader, an author's ideas and intentions are temporarily deferred, only to be reappropriated later when the addressee is present to receive the intended meaning. Condillac argues that an author's original intention is characterized in terms of presence, identity and originality, while writing is characterized in terms of absence, difference and repetition. It is Condillac's emphasis on absence, however, that particularly interests Derrida.

In order to function, writing is structured by absence in two ways. First, writing must always be able to function in the absence of a determinate addressee. If someone writes a letter to someone else who subsequently dies, the letter would continue to be legible despite the death or absence of the addressee. When Derrida wrote "Signature Event Context" he addressed it to a determinate audience, but if no one were ever to read it, it would nonetheless be legible; it would still function as writing. A writing that would not be able to function in the absence of an addressee would not be writing at all. Similarly, a written text must be able to function in the absence of its author. If the author of the letter were to die, again the letter would still be legible. A written text will continue to function, will continue to lend itself to interpretation, regardless of the presence or absence of its addressee or the animating intention of its author.

Of course, the claim that a text can continue to lend itself to interpretation in the absence of an author or a determinate reader is not especially interesting. Obviously a text can be read in the absence of its author and interpreted in ways other than the author intended. But according to the traditional viewpoint, the fact that an author is no longer present to safeguard the meaning of his text does not mean that misinterpretation is inevitable. If we want to know the real meaning of a text, we just have to interpret it in the context of the author's original intention and let its truth come to light.

When we read Plato's *Phaedrus*, for example, clearly Plato does not need to be present in order for the text to be legible. But just because Plato himself is absent does not mean we are condemned to erroneous interpretations and misunderstandings. According to the proponents of the teleology of memory, the fact that there is a temporal distance of some 2,400 years between Plato and his contemporary readers is merely accidental, a provisional obstacle that can be overcome. By reading Plato's text "correctly", we can surmount this temporal distance and literally resurrect the presence of Plato's original intention.

According to Derrida, however, absence is not an accidental predicate that just happens to befall the presence of an original intention. The possibility of a text being reinterpreted in the absence of its author is already contained *within* the original intention itself:

> Therefore, I ask the following question: is this general possibility necessarily that of a failure or trap into which language might *fall,*

> or in which language might lose itself, as if in an abyss situated outside or in front of it ... Or indeed is this risk, on the contrary, its internal and positive condition of possibility? This outside its inside? The very force and law of its emergence? (M: 325)

We can never recollect the presence of an original intention, because there never was an original presence to begin with.

All presence is marked by traces of absence. It is always marked by the no-longer of the past, and the not-yet of the future. And it is only on the basis of these traces that we can experience "presence" at all. So even if we were in the presence of Plato when he wrote the *Phaedrus*, even if we witnessed the original dialogue itself, our experiences would only be partial and incomplete; they too would be marked by the traces of absence and loss. Just as speech requires writing in order to be what it is, so too we can have no experience of presence or anything else without difference, deferral and repetition.

In "Signature Event Context", Derrida uses the term "iterability" to account for this impossible relation. Derrida coined the term from the Sanskrit "*itara*", meaning "other". Normally we are used to seeing the word "iteration" as part of the word "*re*iteration". To reiterate something is to repeat it, and repetition is always the repetition of the same. Iterability also means repetition, but repetition with a difference (*itara*). It is not the simple repetition of the same but a repetition that always has the potential to produce something new. Writing, therefore, is iterable. As soon as an intention is expressed in writing it is always possible that it can be repeated and reinterpreted. But as we have seen, writing is always already *inside* intentionality and presence. We can have no experience at all without this possibility of repetition.

The only way we can ever recognize or comprehend a word, for example, is if it is possible to repeat it. Imagine a word that could only be uttered once. If this were the case, how could we possibly know, say or think it? The only way it could appear on the radar of human comprehension, the only way we could think it at all, is if it contains within it the possibility of its repetition. Even if someone were to exclaim a "unique" idiomatic utterance, the only way it could have a meaning for us, (even if we cannot be sure what the meaning is), is if it can be repeated. But to say that something can be repeated is to say that it can function in the *absence* of an original presence. And this possibility of repetition – which is also the possibility of reinterpretation – is contained within experience itself.

In Chapter 1 we saw how the very possibility of identity is the simultaneous impossibility of identity ever reaching completion. Similarly, we can see now how the very possibility of a word having a meaning is the impossibility of it having a single univocal meaning. Any meaning or identity always contains within itself the possibility of its being repeated and reinterpreted otherwise. This means that the original animating intention of an author can never guarantee the meaning of a text. The very possibility of a text having meaning is the simultaneous impossibility of this guarantee. To return to our Plato example, deferral and repetition were already at the heart of his original intentions when he wrote his dialogues. If they were not, it would not have been possible for Plato to think or write them. Derrida's point, again, is that these grammatological predicates – difference, deferral, repetition – are not accidental; they are not temporary obstacles that can be overcome. They are the necessary conditions of all meaningful experience, and if we have any interest in language, meaning and communication we have a responsibility to give an account of this.

An original animating intention, therefore, is never simply *present*, either within a text or at the moment of its "original" conception. Plato, of course, had specific intentions when he wrote his dialogues, but Derrida's point is that the possibility of these intentions being repeated and reinterpreted in his absence was already there from the moment of their birth. But this does not mean that "anything goes" when it comes to interpretation. We should always strive to comprehend as best we can the intentions of an author. Derrida's own books are written in a determinate context with determinate intentions, which he hopes the reader will take the time to comprehend.[11] But this does not rule out the possibility that the reader may "mis-comprehend" Derrida's own words in a context he himself never intended (something he was accustomed to). To return to our performance of *Hamlet*, the meaning and intention of "Break a leg!" can easily be agreed on. But this does not exclude the possibility that Polonius might leave the theatre in an ambulance. While we all may be able to agree on the meaning of a statement in a given context, its meaning can never be *absolutely* guaranteed.

Différance and iterability both account for the fact that identity is always divided in itself. It is spatially divided in that its identity is the effect of a differential play of traces, and it is temporally divided as its "presence" is marked by traces of absence; the possibility of its full and total recollection is always interminably deferred.

Derrida and Oxford

In the final part of "Signature Event Context", Derrida engages the work of the British philosopher of language J. L. Austin. Austin's most influential text is a series of lecture course notes that were published posthumously in 1961 under the title *How to do Things with Words*. In this text Austin argues for an approach to language that would determine the meaning of words by their use. According to Austin, philosophers of language have traditionally focused their efforts on what he terms "constative utterances". A constative utterance is a statement of fact or state of affairs that possesses a truth-value: it is either true or false. Austin, however, focuses his attentions on "performative utterances" or "speech acts".

A speech act is not a simple description of facts, but is itself the performance of some action. Take a marriage ceremony, for example. When the bride or groom says "I do", the meaning of this utterance is a performance, in this case the agreement to enter into the contract of marriage. It does not derive its meaning from anything beyond or external to itself. A speech act is used not to state that one is doing something, but to actually do it.

Derrida is particularly interested in two points in Austin's speech-act theory. First, according to Austin, all speech acts (or acts of locution) contain within themselves a certain "transformative force". A speech act such as "do your homework", for example, contains within it the possibility of transforming a certain situation (getting someone to do their homework): "it produces or transforms a situation, it operates, and if it can be said that a constative utterance also effectuates something and always transforms a situation, it cannot be said that this constitutes its internal structure, its manifest function or destination, as in the case of the performative" (M: 321). For Austin this possibility of transformation is not something that is added to a speech act, but rather, it is contained *within* it. The second point that interests Derrida is Austin's claim that the possible failure of a speech act – the risk that it may fail to communicate and be misinterpreted – is also contained *within* the speech act itself.

Austin's notions of "transformative force" and "possible failure" bear a striking resemblance to Derrida's notion of iterability. They bear witness to the fact that a speech act always contains within itself the possibility of repetition and reinterpretation. However, Derrida argues that, having opened up the possibility of these questions, Austin backs away from the consequences of his own position: "Austin does not ask himself what consequences derive from the fact that something possible – a possible risk – is always possible, is somehow a necessary possibility" (M: 323–4). Whereas Derrida attempts to give an account of this possibility, Austin simply repeats the Platonic gesture whereby the possibility of repetition and reinterpretation is excluded from the living presence of an original intention. Austin argues that the true meaning of a speech act can always be re-established by referring to what he terms the "total context" of a situation: the presence of the conscious animating intention of a speaking subject, which guarantees the "correct" meaning of any performative.

What fascinates Derrida about Austin is that he is a thinker both of the catastrophe *and* the teleology of memory. At key points in Austin's analysis he emphasizes the fact that all speech acts are contaminated by the risks of possible failure, but at the same time, he continually reduces these risks to the authority and *telos* of an original intention.[12] One of the ways in which Austin attempts to do this is in his distinguishing "ordinary" and "parasitic" language. By ordinary language Austin means our everyday use of language when we say what we mean and know what we mean to say. By parasitic, Austin means the "infelicities" of language – poetry, literature, and so on – that are characterized by the qualities that are normally assigned to writing: difference, deferral and repetition. But rather than account for the fact that these same qualities are always already inside ordinary language, as Austin himself concedes – "as *utterances* our performances are also heir to certain other kinds of ill which infect *all* utterances" (Austin 1962: 21–2; quoted in M: 324, Derrida's emphasis) – he attempts to banish from the purity of ordinary language everything he considers parasitic: "the agony of language that must be kept at a distance" (M: 324). So while he claims to describe the acts and events of ordinary language, Austin in fact makes us accept as "ordinary" a distinct teleological and ethical determination. The *telos* or end of ordinary language is the self-presence and transparency of an original intention. The ethical determination is the designation as "abnormal" and "parasitical" the very infelicities that, as Austin himself recognizes, are a structural possibility of all utterances in general.

> For finally, is not what Austin excludes as anomalous, exceptional, "non-serious," that is, citation (on the stage, in a poem, or in a soliloquy), the determined modification off a general citationality – or rather, a general iterability – without which there would not even be a "successful" performative? Such that – a paradoxical, but inevitable consequence – a successful performative is necessarily an "impure" performative, to use the word that Austin will employ later on when he recognizes that there is no "pure" performative.
>
> (M: 325)

Derrida then turns from the side of failure to that of "positive possibility". Surely there are performatives that do succeed: singular speech acts where the question of possible failure is not an issue? If a friend had entered the room as you were reading this book, asked you what you were reading, and you replied "I am reading a book on Jacques Derrida", would this not be an example of a successful speech act that would contradict Derrida's possible failure thesis? Derrida would agree that this would indeed be a successful speech act, but he argues that it would be a mistake to consider it a success as a result of *opposing* it to the general law of iterability. The failure or success of an individual speech act is always determined by its context, which is what Austin means by the "relative purity" of performatives.

Whether or not a speech act is successful is determined according to other possible speech acts in the same context. Derrida's point is that we must not make the mistake of falling into the trap of opposing successful speech acts, which we have all the time, to the law of iteration in general. If you intended to say you were reading a book on Derrida but instead uttered the words "I am reading *Fly-fishing* by J. R. Hartley", then this would be a failed speech act. But the very possibility of either of these performatives is the law of iterability. You could not have a successful speech act if it did not contain within itself the possibility of its failure (being reinterpreted otherwise).

The law of iterability does not in any way deny the possibility of successful speech acts and intentions (it is what makes them possible), but merely challenges the presupposition of the abiding presence of an animating intention (*telos*), which could always *guarantee* the certainty of any event or context:

> In this typology, the category of intention will not disappear; it will have its place, but from this place it will no longer be able to govern the entire scene and the entire system of utterances. Above all, one would then be concerned with different types of marks or chains of iterable marks, and not with an opposition between citational statements on the one hand, and singular and original-statements-events on the other. (M: 326)

For Derrida, therefore, all language is subject to the law of iterability as the law of possible failure. Austin's attempt to make a clear distinction between "ordinary" language and "parasitic" language, or between "real" language use and literary or artistic language use cannot hold. This is why Derrida problematizes the allegedly clear-cut distinction between philosophy and literature. Derrida never suggests that philosophy and literature are interchangeable, that they are one and the same; rather, Derrida takes account of the general law of iterability, which makes the philosophy–literature distinction possible while rendering impossible the attempt to absolutely safeguard the purity of either one from the other.[13]

Derrida finishes "Signature Event Context" with an analysis of Austin's Fifth Lecture, in which Austin discusses the status of the *signature*. In the Fifth Lecture Austin proceeds to justify why he has favoured the forms of the first-person present indicative in the active voice of the performative. The success of these performatives is safeguarded, according to Austin, by reference to the *source* of the utterance. Austin believes that the source of an oral statement in the active voice is present in the utterance itself, and he believes there is a similar link to the source in a *written* utterance in the form of the signature. Derrida quotes Austin:

> Where there is *not*, in the verbal formula of the utterance, a reference to the person doing the uttering, and so the acting, by means of the pronoun "I" (or by his personal name), then in fact he will be "referred to" in one of two ways: (a) In verbal utterances, *by his being person who does* the uttering – what we may call the utterance-origin which is used generally in any system of verbal reference-co-ordinates. (b) In written utterances (or "inscriptions"), *by his appending his signature* (this has to be done because, of course, written utterances are not tethered to their origin in the way spoken ones are). (Austin 1962: 60–61; quoted in M: 328)

A written signature implies the actual non-presence of the signer. But, according to Austin, the signature contains within itself the presence of the signer as having been present in a past now. With obvious echoes of Plato and Hegel, Austin argues that this original animating presence will continue to accompany the written signature as a guarantee of its original source and meaning intention. The signature can at all times reproduce the originality of this pure event.

Derrida questions whether this is in fact the case. As a written mark, is the signature not also subject to the law of iteration? Are there signatures?

> Yes, of course, every day. The effects of signatures are the most ordinary thing in the world. The condition of possibility for these effects is simultaneously, once again, the condition of their impossibility, of the impossibility of their rigorous purity. In order to function, that is, in order to be legible, a signature must have a repeatable, iterable, imitable form; it must be able to detach itself from the present and singular intention of its production. (M: 328)

For Derrida, the signature, like all language, meaning and experience, is subject to the law of iterability. Contrary to Austin, for whom the meaning of a speech act can always be determined in terms of the *telos* of an original intention, Derrida argues that the very possibility of a meaningful mark is the impossibility of guaranteeing it a single univocal meaning. The original intention of an author – whether in the form of a signature or a philosophical text – always carries within itself the possibility of its being reinterpreted. If this were not the case, then language could never signify anything at all.

Debates and misconceptions

The publication of "Signature Event Context" resulted in many misconceptions and misrepresentations of Derrida's work. This was clearly in evidence in the exchange between Derrida and the American speech-act theorist John Searle. When "Signature Event Context" was published in English in the American journal *Glyph* in 1977, it was accompanied by a short piece by Searle (who was a student of Austin's at Oxford), claiming to be a response to Derrida's text (Searle 1977). In the same year, and again in the pages of *Glyph*, Derrida published a detailed response to Searle's text entitled "Limited Inc.". Searle never replied to Derrida, but in 1983 in the *New York Review of Books*, he published a review of *On Deconstruction* by Jonathan Culler in which he repeated and intensified many of his original objections.[14]

The Derrida–Searle exchange has had a considerable influence on the reception of Derrida's work in certain sectors of academic life and the popular media. Given that many of Searle's "objections" are simply wild misrepresentations of Derrida's position (indeed many of the "objections" are actually borrowed *from* Derrida's text and then purported to be objections *to* the text), we shall not analyse each and every detail of the exchange, but shall confine ourselves to the points that have resulted in some of the more clichéd misrepresentations of Derrida's work.[15] We shall address the following claims: first, that Derrida argues that writing can only function in the absence of a receiver; secondly, that he confuses iterability with permanence; thirdly, that he denies that writing can communicate an intention; and fourthly, that he fails to understand Austin's distinction between "ordinary" and "parasitic" discourse. Finally, we shall address Searle's *New York Review of Books* article as a means to address some classic falsifications of Derrida's ideas.

Searle's first objection to "Signature Event Context" is the alleged claim that, according to Derrida, writing can only function in the absence of an intended receiver: "The argument is that since writing can and must be able to function in the radical absence of the sender, the receiver, and the context of production, it cannot be the communication of the sender's meaning to the receiver" (Searle 1977: 199). According to this viewpoint, absence is the necessary condition of the possibility of any written communication. Searle begs to differ:

> Is it absence, the absence of the receiver from the sender? Again, clearly not. Writing makes it possible to communicate with an absent receiver, but it is not necessary for the receiver to be absent. Written communication can exist in the presence of the receiver,

as for example, when I compose a shopping list for myself or pass
notes to my companion during a concert or lecture.

(*Ibid.*: 199–200)

This is one of many examples where Searle simply misrepresents the argument of "Signature Event Context". At no time in the essay does Derrida
claim that absence is *necessary* for a written communication to function. It
is difficult to conceive how even Searle could take this seriously. What could
it possibly mean to suggest a form of writing that could only have a meaning if no one is around to receive it? Are we to imagine that when Derrida
wrote the text of "Signature Event Context", and was present (like Searle
with his shopping list) when doing so, that he believed it could only acquire
a meaning when he left the room? Not to mention the fact that "Signature
Event Context" was originally a text that was read and received at a conference in Montreal in 1971, presumably in the presence of Derrida, who
read it, and the conference audience, who received it.

These are some of the rather absurd situations that would follow from the
claim that a written communication can only function in the absence of a
receiver. But Derrida says no such thing. The argument of "Signature Event
Context" is not that it is *necessary* for a receiver to be absent for a written
communication to function, but that it is always *possible* for a written communication to function in the absence of an intended receiver.

Derrida wrote "Signature Event Context" in order to communicate a
determinate meaning to a determinate audience. Derrida's point is that the
possibility of his text being interpreted in the absence of this audience is
always a necessary possibility that is inscribed within the written mark itself.
Searle has simply confused necessity with probability. It is always possible
that a text will continue to function in the absence of the intended receiv-
ers. And this rule of iterability applies just as much to a note that one might
write to oneself, such as a shopping list, as it does to a text written explicitly
for a public audience:

> The "shopping list for myself" would be neither producible nor
> utilizable, it would not be what it is nor could it even exist, were
> it not possible for it to function, from the very beginning, in the
> absence of sender and of receiver: that is, of *determinate, actually
> present* senders and receivers. And *in fact* the list cannot function
> unless these conditions are met.   (LI: 49)

Derrida never argues that absence is necessary for a written text to function.
Derrida's point is simply that it is always possible that a written communication can function in the absence of a *determinate* receiver: the original

readers of "Signature Event Context", for example. And the possibility is structurally inscribed within any form of communication.

It is precisely this structural possibility that needs to be accounted for. If, as both Austin and Searle themselves concede, the risk of possible failure is a structural possibility of all speech acts, then this possible failure cannot be dismissed as an empirical accident. If we want to be able to account for the possibility of successful speech acts or "ordinary" language use and so on, then we have to take account of this possibility. How are successful speech acts possible? How is it possible for speech acts to fail? But Searle appears to have no interest in asking these questions.

Searle's second objection is that, in his treatment of the distinction between speech and writing, Derrida confuses iterability with permanence:

> [F]or the purposes of this discussion the most important distin-
> guishing feature is the (relative) permanence of the written text
> over the spoken word ... Now the first confusion that Derrida
> makes, and it is important for the argument that follows, is that
> he confuses iterability with the permanence of the text. He thinks
> the reason that I can read dead authors is because their works are
> repeatable or iterable. Well, no doubt the fact that different copies
> are made of their books makes it a lot easier, but the phenomenon
> of the survival of the text is not the same as the phenomenon of
> repeatability ... This confusion of permanence with iterability lies
> at the heart of his argument ... (Searle 1977: 200)

Derrida never equates repetition or iterability with permanence. He agrees with Searle that "the survival of the text is not the same as the phenomenon of repeatability" (*ibid.*). But for Derrida the latter is the condition of the former. As we have seen, iterability is the very possibility of any "permanence", any "identity" or form of "presence".

Searle has confused iterability – which always involves repetition with the possibility of difference and alteration – with repetition as the simple reproduction of the same, which is why he equates repetition with permanence. But as we have seen since the opening pages of this book, it is precisely this "permanence" or "presence" that Derrida is calling into question. Iterability is not the repetition of the same, but the very condition of the possibility of the "same". As Derrida makes very clear in "Signature Event Context", iterability structures not only written communication, but oral communication, the event and experience in general. How then can Searle claim that for Derrida iterability is equated with permanence? How could "permanence" be attributed to an oral communication or a singular event?

Searle's third objection to Derrida's overall project is his claim that Derrida denies that writing can communicate an intention. According to Searle's Derrida, intentionality is absent from all written communication:

> I have left the most important issue in this section until last. Do the special features of writing determine that there is some break with the author's intentions in particular or with intentionality in general in the forms of communication that occur in writing? Does the fact that writing can continue to function in the absence of the writer, the intended receiver, or the context of production show that writing is not a vehicle of intentionality? It seems to me quite plain that the argument that the author and intended receiver may be dead and the context unknown or forgotten does not in the least show that intentionality is absent from written communication; on the contrary, intentionality plays exactly the same role in written as in spoken communication. What differs in the two cases is not the intentions of the speaker but the role of the context of the utterance in the success of the communication.   (Searle 1977: 201)

Derrida is in full agreement with Searle that "intentionality plays exactly the same role in written as in spoken communication". "Signature Event Context" never denies the existence of intentionality. Rather, "What the text questions is not intention or intentionality but their *telos*, which orients and organizes the movement and the possibility of a fulfillment, realization, and *actualization* in a plenitude that would be *present* to and identical with itself" (LI: 56).

Derrida never denies the existence of intentionality. He merely accounts for the fact that no intention can ever fulfil itself in the form of an absolute presence, a *telos* that would guarantee the intention in all possible contexts. Intentions are fulfilled all the time. Derrida just accounts for the fact that this fulfilment can never be complete and final. It is a structural necessity of any intention that it may be interpreted otherwise; otherwise it could not function as an intention.

Iterability is not opposed to intention, but accounts for the very possibility of successful intentions ("The category of intention will not disappear, it will have its place"). Again, if before the curtain is raised Gertrude turns to Polonius and says "Break a leg", her intention can be determined according to the context. Derrida's point is just that this intention can never *absolutely* guarantee the meaning of the communication. Polonius could always interpret Gertrude's intention as a threat, and this possibility is not a mistaken or accidental interpretation of an original intention; its possibility is contained within the intention itself.

In the final section of his "Reply", Searle turns to what he terms "Derrida's Austin" to list what he takes to be the "major misunderstandings and mistakes" of Derrida's reading. All of Searle's objections revolve around his claim that Derrida has mistaken Austin's strategic exclusion of "parasitic" speech acts as some kind of ethical–metaphysical exclusion. According to Searle, Derrida's attempt to read into Austin some kind of metaphysical conspiracy is merely Derrida's failure to comprehend that before one can consider "parasitic" speech acts one has to first consider the "ordinary", "non-parasitic" acts on which the former depend.

> The existence of the pretended form of the speech act is logically dependent on the possibility of the nonpretended speech act in the same way that any pretended form of behavior is dependent on non-pretended forms of behavior, and in that sense the pretended forms are *parasitical* on the nonpretended forms.   (Searle 1977: 205)

Derrida's mantra throughout the debate, however, is that the possibility of parasitism, of any communication being interpreted otherwise is, as Austin and Searle *themselves* concede, inherent within the structure of all forms of intentionality–communication–speech acts and so on.

You cannot, even strategically or provisionally, exclude the "parasitical" from the "ordinary". They go hand in hand. If you want to take account of the "ordinary", you can only do so by simultaneously taking account of the "parasitical". How could we even identify an "ordinary" speech act if we could not already distinguish it from a "parasitical" one? As Derrida writes:

> Translated into the code of Austin or Searle, *Sec*'s ["Signature Event Context"] question is, in a word, the following: if what they call the "standard," "fulfilled," "normal," "serious," "literal," etc. is *always capable* of being affected by the non-standard, the "void," the "abnormal," the "nonserious," the "parasitical" etc., what does that tell us about the former?   (LI: 89)

To attempt to exclude, even strategically, the "non-serious" from the "serious" is to, as it were, "throw the baby out with the bath water". It is to deprive oneself of the very object that one purports to be analysing. This is also at the root of Searle's objection that "Signature Event Context" argues that the "phenomenon of citationality" is "the same as the phenomenon of parasitic discourse". Derrida responds:

> What *Sec* was driving at, without confusing citationality with parasitism (or fiction, literature, or theatre), was *the possibility they*

have in common: the iterability which renders possible both the "normal" rule or convention and its transgression, transformation, simulation, or imitation. From this, *Sec* drew consequences different from those drawn by Austin; above all, the illegitimate and unfeasible character of the exclusions proposed either on strategic grounds or on methodological (idealizing) ones.

(LI: 98, emphasis added)

In the same way that the *pharmakon* is not the same as writing, but accounts for what speech and writing have in common, or that *différance* is not the same as difference, but accounts for what identity and difference have in common, so too iterability accounts for the very possibility of both "ordinary" and "parasitic" discourse while reducible to neither one nor the other.[16]

Searle also claims that Derrida has fundamentally misunderstood Austin given the former's alleged attempt to impose a moral judgement on the latter's use of the term "parasitical":

Derrida supposes that the term "parasitic" involves some kind of moral judgment: that Austin is claiming that there is something bad or anomalous or not "ethical" about such discourse. Again, nothing could be further from the truth. The sense in which, for example, fiction is parasitic on nonfiction is the sense in which the definition of the rational numbers in number theory might be said to be parasitic on the definition of the natural numbers, or the notion of one logical constant in a logical system might be said to be a parasitic on another, because the former is defined in terms of the latter. Such parasitism is a relation of logical dependence; it does not imply any moral judgment and certainly not that the parasite is somehow sponging off the host … (Searle 1977: 205)

Derrida never accuses Austin of making a "moral judgement" *per se* with regard to parasitic discourse (he does argue that Austin's position presupposes a determinate ethical decision, which is not the same thing), but he nonetheless questions how Searle can claim to appeal to an impartial and objective "logical dependence" when his analysis relies so much on pejorative value judgements:

How is it possible to ignore that this axiology, in all of its systematic and dogmatic insistence, determines an object, the analysis of which is in essence not "logical," objective, or impartial? The axiology involved in this analysis is not intrinsically determined by considerations that are merely logical. What logician, what theoretician in general, would have dared to say: B depends logically on A, therefore B is parasitic, nonserious, abnormal, etc.? One can assert of anything whatsoever that it is "logically depend-ent" without immediately qualifying it (as though the judgment were analytical, or even tautological) with all those attributes, the lowest common denominator of which is evidently a pejorative value judgment. (LI: 92)

Searle cannot avoid this axiology by appealing to a neutral and objective "logical dependence". In fact, as far as Derrida is concerned, it is precisely this "logic" that needs to be called into question:

Logic, the logical, the *logos* of logic cannot be a decisive instance here: rather, it constitutes the object of the debate, the phenomenon that must first be explained before it can be accepted as the decid-ing instance. The matter we are discussing here concerns the value, possibility, and system of what is called logic in general. The law and the effects with which we have been dealing, those of iterabil-ity for example, govern the possibility of every logical proposition, whether considered as a speech act or not. No constituted logic nor any rule of a logical order can, therefore, provide a decision or impose its norms upon these prelogical possibilities of logic. Such possibilities are not "logically" primary or secondary with regard to other possibilities, nor logically primary or secondary with regard to logic itself. (LI: 92–3)

There is no suggestion here that we do away with logic; quite the contrary, in fact. Derrida demands that we give an account of these "prelogical pos-sibilities of logic", that they "be explained before [they] can be accepted". It is precisely at the level of these "prelogical possibilities of logic" that Derrida discerns what he believes to be the distinct ontological decision of Western metaphysics – the *telos* of presence and full recollection: "And this is not just *one* metaphysical gesture among others, it is *the* metaphysical exigency, that which has been the most consistent, the most profound and most potent" (LI: 93). And this logic, which is simply assumed in Western philosophy from Plato to Searle, also commits to an ethical decision, in that it always establishes hierarchical relations between different terms: writing is para-sitic to speech, the outside is parasitic to the inside, difference is parasitic to identity and so on:

The hierarchical axiology, the ethical-ontological distinctions which do not merely set up value-oppositions clustered around an ideal and unfindable limit, but moreover *subordinate* these values to each other (normal/abnormal, standard/parasite, fulfilled/void, serious/nonserious, literal/nonliteral, briefly positive/negative and ideal/nonideal); and in this, whether [Searle] likes it or not, there is metaphysical pathos (infelicity, nonserious, etc. ...).   (LI: 93)

In the "Afterword" to *Limited Inc.*, Gerald Graff puts it to Derrida that many of his critics accuse him of projecting this alleged "metaphysical decision" onto the origins of meaning, language and philosophy. According to these commentators, Derrida is responsible for imposing a kind of "all or nothing", of reducing meaning to a pure self-presence on the one hand and an unlimited free-play or undecidability on the other. According to this argument, the "metaphysical decision" that Derrida discerns in language is only what Derrida himself has projected onto it.

In response, Derrida argues that, "The 'all or nothing' choice was not 'set up' by me" (LI: 120). Whether we like it or not, all conceptualization presupposes this "all or nothing". Any concept that lays claim to any rigour whatsoever, whether in philosophy, in the sciences or anywhere else, presupposes this "all or nothing". The only way a concept can have a rigorous identity and meaning is if it clearly demarcates itself from everything it is not. Even the concept of "difference of degree" *qua* concept presupposes this logic of "all or nothing", of yes or no: differences of degree *or* nondifference of degree.

This is why Derrida finds it "incomprehensible" when, in the course of his *New York Review of Books* article, Searle accuses Derrida of the "assumption that unless a distinction can be made rigorous and precise, it isn't really a distinction at all" (Searle 1993: 182). But what, Derrida asks, would a conceptual distinction possibly be that *would not* be "rigorous and precise"?

What philosopher ever since there were philosophers, what logician ever since there were logicians, what theoretician ever renounced this axiom: in the order of concepts (for we are speaking here of concepts and not of the colors of clouds or the taste of certain chewing gum), when a distinction cannot be rigorous or precise, it is not a distinction at all.   (LI: 123)

The irony here is that the entire edifice of Searle's own discourse is founded on such rigorous distinctions. If Searle seriously wanted to challenge the necessity of these distinctions then his own project would "melt away like snow in the sun" (LI: 124).

All distinctions, relations, oppositions or concepts that lay claim to any rigour whatsoever presuppose the logic of this "all or nothing". And Derrida is bound to this logic as much as anyone else. As we saw in our reading of Saussure, all identity gathers itself to itself ("all") only by differentiating itself from everything it is not ("nothing"). And this movement always follows a circular trajectory. Speech, for example, must pass through writing in order to resurrect itself in its originary presence. But, according to Derrida, the philosophical tradition has always interpreted the circular movement of this economy in terms of a distinct ethico-teleological decision, which attempts to exclude the "nothing" from the purity of the "all".

The tradition always privileges the "all" over the "nothing". Derrida, on the other hand, thinks this logic in terms of the work of mourning. When we mourn we desire both to keep ("all") and let go ("nothing"), and this mourning-work can be reduced to neither one nor the other. Similarly, when it comes to this logic (which is inescapable) Derrida desires both the "all" and the "nothing", while reducing its circular movement to neither one nor the other. Just like speech and writing, the "all" and the "nothing" are always interwoven with each other. You cannot have one without the other.

This works both ways. One cannot simply privilege the "nothing" over the "all" either. One cannot simply extricate writing, difference and absence from speech, identity and presence – something Derrida has often been accused of. We could not even conceive of the former without taking account of their relationships to the latter.

Take the concept "truth". According to Derrida, "truth", like every other concept, presupposes the "all or nothing". The problem is that philosophers have always attempted either to completely immunize the "all" from the "nothing", or to do the exact opposite. Plato is an example of the former. He attempts to safeguard the purity of truth from everything it is not (difference, deferral and death). In so doing he repeats the classic logic of privileging the "all" over the "nothing".

An example of the second attempt would be recent trends in so-called "postmodernism". According to these arguments, we can simply deny the existence of the "all" altogether. It is not uncommon in these circles to hear people deny the existence of "truth", "reason" or "identity", and to privilege instead "difference", "multiplicity", "indeterminacy" and so on. But according to Derrida this is just to reverse the "all or nothing", privileging the latter over the former. For the same reason that one cannot take account of the "all" without the "nothing", so too one cannot take account of the "nothing" without the "all". That is why relativism, for example, is a contradictory position. Relativism denies the existence of absolutes, claiming that meaning is relative to different languages and cultures. It denies the "all" (absolutes) and privileges the "nothing" (relative differences). But in order to have any conceptual coherence, relativism has to presuppose precisely the "all" that it claims to oppose. You can only conceptualize relative differences *in terms of* absolutes.[17]

Derrida has therefore never aligned himself with those who claim to do away with "truth", "reason" and "logic". Truth is not a mere metaphor or theoretical fiction for Derrida. It is not an unfortunate by-product of modernism that we would be better off without: "we cannot and we must not forego the *Aufklärung* [Enlightenment], in other words, what imposes itself as the enigmatic desire for vigilance, for lucid vigil, for elucidation, for critique and truth" (N: 195). We could not even conceive of concepts such as "difference" and "multiplicity" without *some* conception of identity and truth.

Continuing his "logical dependence" argument, Searle goes on to claim that Derrida falsely equates the sense in which fiction is parasitic on nonfiction with the sense that writing is parasitic on speech:

> But these are quite different. In the case of the distinction between fiction and nonfiction, the relation is one of *logical dependency*. One could not have the concept of fiction without the concept of serious discourse. But the dependency of writing on spoken language is a *contingent fact* about the history of human languages and not a logical truth about the nature of language.
>
> (Searle 1977: 207)

But Derrida never attributes a relation of logical dependence to speech and writing. His point is that both the speech–writing relation and the allegedly logical relation of non-fiction and fiction both presuppose the logic of the "all or nothing". Both speech and non-fiction are idealized in such a way as to exclude everything that does not belong to them (writing and fiction). But, as Austin himself concedes, we cannot exclude the non-fictional from the fictional, the non-serious from the serious. The possibility of one necessarily implies the possibility of the other. It is a two-way street:

> When [Searle] writes: "One could not have the concept of fiction without the concept of serious discourse," one could with equal legitimacy reverse the order of dependence. This order is not a one-way street (how can the serious be defined or postulated without reference to the nonserious, even if the latter is held to be simply external to it?) and everything that claims to base itself upon such a conception disqualifies itself immediately. (LI: 104)

Searle's entire argument presupposes precisely these "all or nothing" one-way streets. Derrida is merely pointing out that these conceptual distinctions work both ways. The "all" is always inhabited by the "nothing" and vice versa. Derrida's aim in "Signature Event Context" is to give an account of this mutual contamination.

In his *New York Review of Books* article, Searle appeals to other notorious misreadings of Derrida that would be useful to address here. According to Searle, Derrida is guilty of the claim "that all we think of as meaningful language is just a free play of signifiers or an endless process of grafting texts onto texts" (1993: 171). This is the classic misrepresentation of Derrida as advocating the absolute indeterminacy of meaning. According to this caricature, Derrida argues that all meanings are essentially indeterminate. In any given context any meaning is as good as any other.

First, Derrida has never claimed that meaning is subject to an infinite "free play" of language or that all meaning is indeterminate. Derrida makes a clear distinction between indeterminacy of meaning and undecidablity of meaning. All meaning is structured, as we have seen, by the necessary possibility of its being interpreted otherwise. But this does not mean that it necessarily *will* be interpreted otherwise, and it certainly does not mean that meaning is indeterminate. To say that meaning is structured by undecidablity is just to accept the fact that any meaningful mark can always be possibly reinterpreted in a different context. But this does not mean that a meaningful mark has no determinate meaning in a *given* context.

> I do not believe I have ever spoken of "indeterminacy," whether in regard to "meaning" or anything else. Undecidability is something else again. ... [I] want to recall that undecidability is always a determinate oscillation between possibilities (for example of meaning, but also of acts). These possibilities are themselves highly determined in strictly defined situations (for example, discursive – syntactical or rhetorical – but also political, ethical, etc.) They are pragmatically determined. The analyses that I have devoted to undecidability concern just these determinations and these definitions, not at all some vague "indeterminacy." (LI: 148)

There is no such thing as "indeterminacy of meaning" or an "infinitely interpretable text" for Derrida. All texts are finite and determinate. We can, however, attempt to loosen up the determinacy of a particular text by attuning our reading to the points of undecidability, which resist the attempts of any determinate author or reader to decide its meaning once and for all. But that does not mean we can read whatever we like into it. We have to respect the fact that a text is *this* particular text. So while we may be able to discern a certain undecidability at work in Plato's *Phaedrus*, for example, that does not mean that we can reinterpret the text however we like. In any given context one interpretation is *not* as good as any other. This basic misunderstanding has often resulted in the charge that Derrida's own texts must be indeterminate and infinitely interpretable. To this accusation, Derrida responds:

> For of course there is a "right track," a better way, and; let it be said in passing how surprised I have often been, how amused or discouraged, depending on my humor, by the use or abuse of the following argument: Since the deconstructionist (which is to say, isn't it, the skeptic–relativist–nihilist!) is supposed not to believe in truth, stability, or the unity of meaning, in intentions or "meaning-to-say," how can he demand of us that we read *him* with pertinence, precision, rigor? How can he demand that his own text be interpreted correctly? How can he accuse anyone else of having misunderstood, simplified, deformed it, etc.? In other words, how can he discuss, and discuss the reading of what he writes? The answer is simple enough: this definition of the deconstructionist is *false* (that's right: false, not true) and feeble; it supposes a bad (that's right: bad, not good) and feeble reading of numerous texts, first of all mine, which therefore must finally be read and reread. Then perhaps it will be understood that the value of truth (and all those values associated with it) is never contested or destroyed in my writings, but only reinscribed in more powerful, larger, more stratified contexts.
>
> (LI: 146)

The indeterminacy of meaning thesis is often mistakenly attributed to Derrida because of confusion over his famous "there is nothing outside the text" (*il n'y a pas de hors-texte*). But all Derrida means by this is that we can never step outside time and history and assume a God's-eye view of the world. We can never appeal to some principle or *telos* outside time that can determine absolutely the context in which we find ourselves. So when we read a philosophical work, for example, we cannot appeal to some *telos* (the author's intention) outside the text that could definitively decide its meaning.

All experience is an effect of differential relations. As we saw with the blind person from our earlier example, the very fabric of experience is an effect of difference and deferral. And this is what Derrida means by "text". Text is not a book, or words on a page, or even language. All identity and language, indeed all meaning and experience, is structured for Derrida as "text", that is, according to the general law of iterability:

> What I call "text" implies all the structures called "real," "economic," "historical," socio-institutional, in short: all possible referents.

Another way of recalling once again that "there is nothing outside the text." That does not mean that all referents are suspended, denied or enclosed in a book, as people have claimed, or have been naive enough to believe and to have accused me of believing. But it does mean that every referent, all reality has the structure of a differential trace, and that one cannot refer to this "real" except in an interpretive experience. The latter neither yields meaning nor assumes it except in a movement of differential referring. That's all.   (LI: 148)

Derrida does *not* claim that we are trapped in language or that all experience is linguistic (whatever that could possibly mean). Derrida never denies the reality of the real world or the possibility of reference.[18] He merely wants to give an account of what our everyday understanding of the "real" presupposes, and attempt to describe the "real" differently. When physicists argue that material objects are in fact immaterial waves of energy or subatomic articles spinning around in a vacuum, they do not deny the reality of the material world. They merely attempt to redescribe how we think about the "material" in a description that they believe to be more comprehensive and useful.

Similarly, Derrida never denies the "real world", or "facts", or "objectivity". Like the physicists, he attempts to redescribe these concepts in a more comprehensive and useful manner. His point is just that their meaning is always determined according to a determinate context:

What is called "objectivity," scientific for instance (in which I firmly believe, in a given situation), imposes itself only within a context which is extremely vast, old, powerfully established, stabilized or rooted in a network of conventions (for instance, those of language) and yet which still remains a context. And the emergence of the value of objectivity (and hence of so many others) also belongs to a context. We can call "context" the entire "real-history-of-the-world," if you like, in which this value of objectivity and, even more broadly, that of truth (etc.) have taken on meaning and imposed themselves. That does not in the slightest discredit them. In the name of what, of which other "truth," moreover, would it? One of the definitions of what is called deconstruction would be the effort to take this limitless context into account, to pay the sharpest and broadest attention possible to context, and thus to an incessant movement of recontextualization.   (LI: 136)

Just because Derrida argues that "truth" is contextual does not mean that anything can be considered true in a given context. If we take the following statements "the earth revolves around the sun" and "the sun revolves around the earth" then, according to Derrida, the former is *true* while the latter is *false*. Derrida's point is that we do not have to appeal to some God's-eye point of view (the assumption that we can stand "outside of the text") in order to make this claim. Within the determinate context of the history of science and contemporary common sense, the former of these statements is obviously true and the latter is false. However, the statement "the earth revolves around the sun" does contain within itself, whether we like it or not, the possibility of its being reinterpreted in different contexts. It could be used as a code between CIA agents, for example. Derrida's point again is that all marks contain *within themselves* the possibility of this citation and reinterpretation in different contexts (iterability), and we have to take account of this.

What are we to make of Searle's reading of Derrida? Searle continually accuses Derrida of abandoning all protocols of argument, of academic rigour, "explanatory adequacy" and so on in favour of some wanton playfulness or iconoclasm. But as we have seen, even a cursory reading of "Signature Event Context" would suffice to demonstrate that it is in fact Searle's alleged "objections" that fail to meet the demands of conceptual rigour and argumentation. If Searle had himself lived up to the professional standards he wishes to protect, he could not have possibly signed his name to these two "responses".

Again, let us remind ourselves of the timeline. After Searle published his initial response to "Signature Event Context", Derrida wrote a lengthy and detailed response to each of Searle's objections. To anyone who takes the time to read the exchange it is clear that Searle misrepresents Derrida. What is remarkable is that not only did Searle ignore Derrida's response, but he decided to compound his initial errors by publishing in no less public a forum than the *New York Review of Books*. Why would John Searle, a respected philosopher and university professor, disrespect the very protocols of professional rigour that he wished to represent? While we are not interested in analysing Searle's personal motives or intentions, his reading of Derrida is symptomatic of a rather disturbing ideology within certain academic circles.

The Austrian philosopher Karl Popper famously proposed falsifiability as a means to test a scientific hypothesis or theory. According to Popper, if it was not at least theoretically possible for a theory to be falsified then it was no theory at all, but rather an ideology. Whereas a genuine theory always opens itself up to the possibility of questioning, debate and so on, an ideology is a dogmatically held belief system that attempts to safeguard itself from all forms of questioning and experimentation. For Popper, Freudian psychoanalysis is an example of an ideology. If, for example, someone said to Freud, "Dr Freud, we have noticed a few inconsistencies in your argument" and Freud replied "Ah yes, but that's only because you unconsciously resent me as a father figure", then, according to Popper, this belief system fails the criteria for a genuine theory and takes on the form of an ideology.

Whereas any scientific theory is open to the possibility of falsification, ideology either outright excludes or ignores potential attempts to question it, or, as in the Freud example above, it appropriates the possible falsification as a *confirmation* rather than a problematization of its original position. Either way, ideologies exist solely to reinforce themselves. Many of Derrida's attempts to question the basic presuppositions of philosophy (in particular those of logic, truth, presence, etc.) have often provoked reactions that can only be described as ideological. As we have seen in the case of Searle, Derrida's actual arguments are either completely ignored, or they are appropriated in the form of straw men – "Derrida says there is no truth", "Derrida claims we are trapped in language", "All meaning is relative" and so on – as a means to *confirm* precisely what Derrida is calling into question.

Many have reacted to Derrida's attempts to question the basic presuppositions of their positions by either misrepresenting his arguments or by completely ignoring him (Searle does both). In these cases, all claims or pretence to academic rigour, not to mention professional courtesy, are simply dropped. Indeed, in the attempt to safeguard the purity of their own presuppositions from all questioning, many of the self-professed academic thought-police have willingly and enthusiastically endorsed outright dogma and censorship.

Such was arguably the ideological fervour that led to the unfortunate events of 1992, when a band of academic crusaders attempted (and failed) to influence and deter the decision of the University of Cambridge to award Derrida an honorary degree. After the university ballot Derrida was awarded the degree, but at the time the incident created quite a stir and much bad blood in academic life. But all this paled in comparison to the actions of Ruth Barcan Marcus of Yale University, who attempted to intervene in the decision of the French government to appoint Derrida the Director of the International College of Philosophy in Paris. The fact that this was the decision of a foreign nation, and that his colleagues had unanimously elected him to this position, not to mention that at the time Derrida was also a visiting professor at Yale (Marcus's own institution), did nothing to deter her efforts.[19]

Derrida and analytic philosophy

Despite the efforts of Searle and Marcus *et al.*, however, a lively debate has emerged in recent years between readers of Derrida and readers of Anglo-

American philosophy. Derrida himself always called for a productive dia-logue between the so-called "continental" and "analytic" traditions. Indeed, while Derrida's texts focus primarily on continental thinkers, he has often described his own reading style as having a lot in common with that of ana-lytic philosophy. Derrida is always trying to determine the limits of certain concepts in texts and to question the very possibility of conceptuality or meaning at all. This is an approach to philosophy that he believes he holds in common with the analytic tradition.

> So: I am an analytic philosopher – a conceptual philosopher. I say this very seriously. That's why there are no fronts. That's what complicates the picture. Because in France, and on the Continent in Europe (indeed, sometimes in England and America) there are many misunderstandings of what I am trying to do, and it's per-haps because I am not simply on the "continental side." Despite a number of appearances, my "style" has something essential to do with a motivation that ones also finds in analytic philosophy, in conceptual philosophy. From that point of view, then, there are no fronts here. I am rather on the side of conceptual philosophy.
> (Derrida, "Response to Moore", in Glendinning 2001: 83–4)

Many of the features of Derrida's thought are also found in the work of many of the key thinkers of the analytic tradition.[20] The problematization of the value of presence, that language can correspond to the world exactly as it is "in itself", or that consciousness and identity are ever simply present and transparent to all, are some of the fundamental questions of analytic thought in the twentieth century.

As Derrida challenges the essentialist pretensions of thinkers such as Plato or Hegel, so too analytic thinkers such as Wilfrid Sellars, Quine, Donald Davidson and, of course, Wittgenstein have all reacted in a similar fashion to the same pretensions in the work of different thinkers. Wittgenstein is a case in point of a thinker who formerly assumed the "all or nothing" dis-tinction between the necessary and the contingent, privileging the former over the latter – central to the work of thinkers such as Frege, Husserl and Russell – only to abandon this distinction in his later work.

The two founding fathers of the modern analytic tradition, Gottlob Frege and Bertrand Russell, both dedicated their lives to grounding science and mathematics on the ahistorical necessary truths of formal logic. This was a classic attempt to derive the contingent from the necessary, the sensible from the intelligible. These necessary rules of logic would be independ-ent of the contingent historical reality of actual existence. The true role of philosophy, according to this line of thinking, is to concentrate on these ahistorical *a priori* eternal truths. With Frege and Russell we encounter the Platonic attempt to separate the realms of the necessary and the contingent, privileging, of course, the former over the latter.

As a young man Wittgenstein set out in his *Tractatus Logico-Philosophicus* (2002) to do just that. In the *Tractatus* Wittgenstein attempts to demonstrate how the meaning of words or sentences is determined according to formal logical rules, which "picture" or "correspond" exactly to things or states of affairs in the world. Wittgenstein's position ran into problems, however, and he eventually abandoned this approach to language and meanings in terms of the necessary–contingent distinction.

Similar to Derrida, the later Wittgenstein no longer holds to the view that language or meaning can absolutely represent the world or a speaker's intentions. Wittgenstein does not claim that language cannot have a determinate meaning; rather, he redescribes the question of meaning in terms of its use in different contexts or what he called "language games". The meaning of a word is determined not by its magical ability to represent logically some entity or states of affairs but according to its use in different determinate contexts.

Wittgenstein's abandonment of the necessary–contingent distinction in favour of a context-based approach to language and meaning has had a considerable influence on subsequent Anglo-American philosophy. In his *Empiricism and the Philosophy of Mind* (1997), for example, Sellars criticizes what he terms "the myth of the given". The myth of the given is just what Derrida and the phenomenological tradition mean by the myth of presence. Both Sellars and Derrida challenge the notion that objects, consciousness and indeed all experience in general are simply given, present and transparent to all. There is no simple unmediated access to presence or to how things "really are".

Two of the philosophers to whom Derrida is often compared are the American philosophers Quine and Davidson. Quine, like Wittgenstein, was formerly an adherent of the Vienna school of logical positivism, which held that all meaningful sentences are either analytic – necessarily true by virtue of their logical form – or synthetic – their truth is determined by appeal to experience and subject to possible revision. This again is the familiar distinction between the necessary and the contingent, which has dominated Western philosophy from Plato and Aristotle to Frege and Russell.

In his 1951 paper "Two Dogmas of Empiricism" (1961), Quine attacks the entrenched dogma of the analytic–synthetic distinction. According to Quine, all meaningful statements derive their truth-value not by virtue of their logical form, or by simply appealing to empirical verification; the truth-values of all meaningful statements are determined according to what Quine calls the "web of belief". A particular statement is held to be true by virtue of its relationship to other statements within the totality of this web of belief. The analytic truths that we hold to be necessarily true are only what we now hold to be true. Their truth-vales are determined according to the value they take relative to our web of beliefs, not according to some logical truths that would be independent of our beliefs.

Take the claim "all bachelors are unmarried men", for example. According to the logical positivists this is an example of an analytic statement because its truth is guaranteed by its logical form: the subject "bachelor" necessarily includes the predicate "unmarried man". But according to Quine the alleged "analyticity" of this statement cannot be accounted for by appeal to some logical truth that is independent of all language use. The reason why people have formerly taken "all bachelors are unmarried men" to be an analytic necessary truth, is because "unmarried man" and "bachelor" are taken to be logically equivalent. But, as Quine points out, the relationship between "bachelor" and "unmarried man" is hardly one of logical equivalence, independent of all conventions of language use. If aliens landed from another planet there is no reason why they would or could logically equate "bachelor" with "unmarried man". Quine's point is that the only reason we can posit such a relation is because of the conventions of language use. The reason that we equate "bachelor" and "unmarried man" is simply a result of how we define the terms according to the conventions of our web of belief. The strict distinction between analytic and synthetic collapses. Similar to Saussure, therefore, Quine believes that the meaning of any intentional statement is always determined according to its position relative to the total system or web of beliefs.

Quine also dismisses the appeal to the intentions of a speaker or an author as a means to guarantee the meaning of a word or statement. He gives the famous example of a "field-linguist" attempting to translate an unknown language. If a native speaker of this language was to point at a rabbit and say "gavagai", we have no guarantee that the native intends to mean or say "rabbit". He could be saying "rabbit", of course, but it is always possible that he is saying something such as "Behold, a rabbit!", or "Food", or "Let's go hunting", or "Temporal cross-section of a four-dimensional space-time extension of a rabbit" and so on. Quine's point is that the meaning of a word or statement cannot be guaranteed by means of ostension (pointing at something) or by speculating about the intention of the one who states it. The only way we could possibly understand what the native means by "gavagai" is if we were to be immersed in the web of *his* beliefs.

This led Quine to his "indeterminacy of translation" thesis. Because the field-linguist and the native share two different webs of belief, it is impossible to translate between the two. The only way the linguist could ever understand the word "gavagai" is by sharing the same web of beliefs as the native. But even if the linguist immerses himself in the native's culture, every utterance he would encounter would similarly be determined by reference to *other* utterances, which are unfamiliar to him.

The upshot of this is that we can no more appeal to the intentions of a speaker than we can to the "logical form" of the language in order to relieve us of our difficulties. Not only are the intentions of the native completely indeterminable for the linguist, but even the intentional content of my own psychological states is subject to indeterminacy. I cannot be certain of the intentions of speakers in my own language nor indeed be certain of the intentional content of my own psychological states.

As far as Quine is concerned, all intentionalist semantics, all attempts to communicate a meaning by means of language, are subject to a fundamental indeterminacy. However, having posited this structural indeterminacy, Quine fails to take account of the inevitable implications of his own argument. He backs away from his own conclusions, content to accept the fact that we nonetheless do seem able to understand each other and our own intentional states. It is important to note a fundamental difference between Derrida and Quine here. Derrida, we remember, never advocates the "indeterminacy of meaning". On the contrary, he argues that meaning is always determined. All meaning is necessarily structured by undecidability, but that is not the same thing as indeterminacy.[21]

Indeed, while Derrida is sympathetic to Quine's attempts to displace the necessary–contingent distinction and the *telos* of an intentionalist semantics, he argues that Quine's epistemological relativism is a contradictory position. According to Quine, both the field-linguist and the native would have their own webs of belief and there would be no way of translating between the two. The claims of each can only be adjudicated *relative* to their own respective "webs of belief". But as we have seen, relativism is a contradictory position, in that it presupposes the "all or nothing" logic that it attempts to refute, and Quine's epistemological relativism is no different. We could not even recognize relative differences or tell them apart unless we had some conception of the "all" as a means to distinguish them. This point is echoed in the work of another American philosopher: Donald Davidson.

Davidson also challenges the alleged claims of language to represent the world or a speaker's intentions exactly as they are "in themselves". Davidson proposes the scheme–content distinction as the "third dogma of empiricism". The scheme–content distinction recurs throughout the history of philosophy as the attempt to determine an ahistorical "scheme" that can be fitted to some actual "content": for example, the many attempts of philosophers to determine how the scheme of language "fits" or represents the content of actual things or states of affairs in the world. The purpose of philosophy then is to separate the scheme from the content, a gesture we have already encountered in the works of Plato, Hegel and others.

We cannot, however, separate the scheme from the content; we cannot separate language from its use. Like Quine, Davidson also argues that intentions or beliefs can never absolutely fix the meaning of an utterance. The meaning of all meaningful statements or utterances is determined by their context. The meaning of any particular belief presupposes "endless interlocking beliefs" (Davidson 1984: 157). We cannot simply separate some theory of language from its use in order to guarantee the meaning of statements. All reality, and all experience, are interpreted. All experience is conceptual.

However, Davidson follows Derrida in noting a fundamental contradiction in Quine's relativist position. How could we possibly even identify and distinguish relative differences if we did not have some sort of point of comparability?

> The dominant metaphor of conceptual relativism, that of differing points of view, seems to betray an underlying paradox. Different points of view make sense, but only if there is a common coordinate system on which to plot them; yet the existence of a common system belies the claim of dramatic incomparability. What we need, it seems to me, is some idea of the considerations that set the limits to conceptual contrast. *(Ibid.: 184)*

The limits to conceptual relativism are what Davidson calls "truth-conditions". Taking Quine's "radical translation" (indeterminacy of meaning), Davidson argues that the field-linguist would not be able even to identify the language of the native *as* different if he could not appeal to some form of truth-conditions as a means to identify and distinguish them. According to Davidson, Quine has things the wrong way around. Truth is a logically primitive notion. It is only by virtue of having some form of truth-conditions that we can identify relative differences in the first place.

Both Derrida and Davidson would agree with Quine that the field linguist could never produce a *guaranteed* univocal word-for-word translation of the native's language. But it does not follow from this that there can be no possibility of communication whatsoever. The very fact that we can identify the native's language *as* a language different from our own presupposes that we can recognize at least a minimal amount of shared truth-conditions – protocols of nomination, grammatical and syntactical structures and so on – that are also presupposed by our language. Indeed, Derrida would argue that not only can the field-linguist never be absolutely sure that he has understood the native, but two English speakers would have the same dilemma. We can never *guarantee* that we have understood the intentional meaning of a fellow English speaker, as we saw with our example of Gertrude and Polonius. But this does not mean that all meaning and all communication are indeterminate. We can still strive to understand each other within determinate contexts. If he invested enough time and effort, even Quine's field-linguist could manage to communicate to some degree with his native friend, because the relative differences ("nothing") of their respective languages presupposes the possibility of some form of shared truth-conditions ("all").

While Derrida and Davidson would differ as to what exactly these truth-conditions might be, they both agree that we cannot accept the "all" as simply given. But both of them insist that we nonetheless need some understanding of truth. Just because they challenge a particular conception of truth does not mean they renounce truth altogether. We cannot escape the economy of the "all or nothing" – we could not have any coherent experience if we did – and, like Davidson, Derrida insists that we give an account of these conditions.

Conclusion

In this chapter we have seen how Derrida subjects many of the classical texts and problems of philosophy to a work of mourning. From Plato to Hegel, and Austin to Searle, philosophers have always understood the question of identity in terms of a teleology of memory. Whether it is living memory or Universal Spirit in Plato and Hegel, or the original animating intention of an author in Austin and Searle, all of these thinkers claim to overcome the "obstacles" of difference, deferral and death. Like the conditional gift, the work of these thinkers follows a circular movement in which the end is always presupposed in the beginning; despite appearances, everything will eventually be gathered into a harmonious whole and all accounts will be settled.

We can never completely recollect the past. Memory is always incomplete: the circle is always cut and we can never exorcise the spectral figures of loss and death. And it is precisely this impossibility of teleological recollection that is the very possibility of speech, communication, meaning and intentionality. So while the teleology of memory always attempts to extricate and purify the necessary (speech, spirit, intention, identity, presence, etc.) from the contingent (writing, iterability, difference, deferral and death), for Derrida the necessary and the contingent, like the all and the nothing, are inextricably interwoven with each other. We cannot have the one without the other. We can never step outside the contingency of history, time and writing. While we passionately desire to recollect and resurrect the past, the most we can do is stitch together the traces and cinders of memory. All of Derrida's neologisms – the *pharmakon*, dissemination, *différance*, iterability – are figures of mourning in that they attempt to give an account of the impossibility of recollection and the teleology of memory, while at the same time accounting for the interminable desire to keep and preserve the past.

Having examined some of Derrida's critical readings of the philosophical tradition, we shall now turn to the influence of psychoanalysis and phenomenology on Derrida's attempt to challenge our conception of identity in terms of the teleology of memory.

CHAPTER THREE

Repetition and post cards: psychoanalysis and phenomenology

In this chapter we shall discuss the considerable influence of Freud, Husserl and Heidegger on the work of Derrida. We cannot underestimate the influence of these three thinkers on Derrida's deconstructive project. Derrida's first writings, his earliest articulation of the problems and questions that would occupy him throughout his life were a direct result of his critical engagement with Husserl's phenomenology, and the figures of Freud and Heidegger recur again and again throughout his work. Indeed, many of Derrida's deconstructive strategies – the trace, difference and deferral, the critique of presence – are prefigured in the works of these seminal thinkers. What particularly interests Derrida is the fact that all three challenge our conception of identity in terms of a teleology of memory. Whereas Plato, Hegel, Searle and Austin all think identity in terms of recollecting a determinate end (*telos*), of gathering the past into a harmonious whole, Freud, Husserl and Heidegger all think the catastrophe of memory in terms of *repetition*. But while Derrida's own conceptions of these themes are firmly rooted in his readings of Freud, Husserl and Heidegger, he argues that each ultimately fails to extricate himself from the circular enclosure of recollection. It is how we think our relation to death, loss and mourning that will determine the distance between Derrida and his illustrious predecessors. While Derrida's texts are littered with the spectral traces of ghosts and phantoms, there is ultimately no sense of mourning in Freud, Husserl or Heidegger.[1] In the end all three attempt to banish and exorcise the ghosts that haunt and disturb our pretensions to harmony and rigorous science.

The post

On a visit to the Bodleian Library in Oxford in 1977, Derrida accidentally discovered a postcard. The postcard in question was a depiction of a representation of Socrates and Plato by Matthew Paris, a thirteenth-century Benedictine monk. That chance finding resulted in a book called *The Post Card: From Socrates to Freud and Beyond*. What fascinated Derrida about Paris's representation is that Socrates is both seated and writing, while Plato stands behind his master, finger outstretched, apparently dictating what is to be written. But this is a complete reversal of the roles of Socrates and Plato that have been handed down to us. As any history or philosophy book will tell you, it was Plato who faithfully transcribed the wisdom of Socrates (who never wrote anything) and not the other way around.

This reversal of the roles of Socrates and Plato, of the one who speaks and the one who writes, illustrates for Derrida the problematic relationship between speech and writing in the history of Western metaphysics. As we saw in Derrida's reading of the *Phaedrus,* Socrates glorifies the virtues of living speech while denigrating the evils of writing, a gesture that, according to Derrida, repeats itself throughout Western history. But as Plato himself concedes, as much as Socrates may have wished to exclude writing from the pure interiority of living speech, he too requires writing to fill the gaps of finite lived memory. Socrates, the great proponent of speech and denouncer of writing, cannot do without writing.

This raises many interesting questions for Derrida. Could it be that Paris simply made a mistake, mislabelling his two protagonists? Or is it possible that this obscure Benedictine monk was himself attempting to challenge the metaphysical tradition handed down to him by these two great Greek philosophers? Derrida uses the postcard as a springboard to pursue a series of provocative philosophical questions. How can we be sure that ancient documents or archives – Plato's dialogues, for example – accurately represent the past as it actually happened? Can we be sure that we have received our traditions and identities in accordance with the original intentions of their originators? How can we be certain that we are the intended recipients? Can we even be sure of the actual authors – Socrates or Plato, for example? Or can we rule out the possibility that there is always more than one author?

Derrida also ponders the very figure of the postcard itself. A postcard is both private and public. One may write a private personal message to a friend or a loved one, but as soon as it enters the postal system, as soon as it is sent, it exposes itself to the all-encompassing gaze of the public. In the figure of the postcard the public space is contaminated by the most intimate and private communications, while this very private space is simultaneously contaminated by everything public. In fact, Derrida's text *The Post Card* is itself a collection of intimate postcards written to a lover. But by virtue of the fact that they are postcards, neither Derrida nor anyone else for that matter can prevent them from being read or interpreted otherwise than their author may have intended. No matter how private they may be, postcards can always be read and reinterpreted by whoever may happen to come upon them.

In Chapter 2 we saw how any communication always includes within it the possibility of its being interpreted otherwise. When an author writes a book, for example, it is always possible that the book can be interpreted in ways the author did not originally intend. And this is no mere accident. The possibility is there as soon as the author puts pen to paper. It is precisely the impossibility of guaranteeing the intended meaning of a communication that makes communication possible in the first place.

Similarly, the very possibility of sending a letter is also the impossibility of guaranteeing that it will always arrive at its intended destination. We all send letters, packages and postcards, and most of the time they arrive at their correct destination. But from the moment we drop a letter in a post box, it is always possible that it may go astray, that it might get "lost in the post". This does not mean, of course, that letters never arrive. As we saw in the debate with Searle, just because it is possible that a letter may go astray does not mean that it necessarily *will* go astray. But this possibility is no mere accident that befalls the otherwise smooth functioning of the postal service. The very act of sending a letter always contains this possibility of *destin-errance*.

Derrida uses this postal metaphor to challenge once again the circular model of economy that determines our traditional conception of identity. In the case of communication, for example, an author has an idea or a thought that they express in the material form of a written or spoken word (speech relies on material sound waves). On receiving this communication, the listener or reader literally receives and resurrects the original meaning in the "dead body of the signifier". The original meaning follows a circular path. Its identity literally goes outside itself via the material signifier only to return to itself in its pristine purity. But as we have seen, the very possibility of this circular model of communication is the impossibility of the circle ever closing in on itself. Death, loss, difference and deferral are always already at work at the heart of an "original" meaning. Something can always escape the powers of recollection. Letters can always get lost in the post.

All of our traditional forms of identity are postal. They literally send or destine themselves to themselves, like a self-addressed envelope. Take a proper name such as "Derrida", for example. As we saw in our reading of Saussure, this name can only assume its sense of identity in a system of differences. To do this it has literally to go outside itself to distinguish itself from everything it is not. In order to have any sense of identity at all, all forms of identity must destine themselves to themselves via this medium of differentiation. So the proper name "Derrida" can only assume its identity by first going outside itself – distinguishing itself from "Berrida", "Gerrida", "Derrisa" and so on – as a means to return to itself and assume its full identity. In the postal economies of Hegel and Plato, the necessity of passing through this system of differences and postal delays is a mere inconvenience of the demands of writing. But, as Derrida argues, these differences, delays and the possibility of loss are built into the postal system itself. Even a proper name can get lost in the post.

The postal metaphor is, therefore, particularly useful for Derrida. It helps us to understand how identities are constituted as a circular movement of sending and receiving. It also illustrates how the very possibility of any identity presupposes the impossibility of guaranteeing that an identity will arrive at its intended destination. The postal metaphor also raises interesting questions about inheritance and the past. What does it mean to inherit or receive a tradition, for example? Can we be sure we have inherited our traditions precisely as our forebears intended? How do we think our relationship to the past? How do we record or archive the past?

Derrida appeals to the postal metaphor to challenge once again the claims of philosophers who think they can cheat the catastrophe of memory and purify identity of difference, deferral and death. In Freud, Husserl and Heidegger, Derrida discovers fellow travellers who also attempt to affirm and account for the fact that the circular movement of recollection never comes to completion. But while all three thinkers have had a considerable influence on how Derrida himself thinks about mourning and loss, Derrida discerns in all three a latent nostalgia for presence and recollection: the secret expectation of receiving a special delivery in the evening post.

Freud and psychoanalysis

In *Of Grammatology*, Derrida claims that the two disciplines most likely to challenge the conception of identity understood in terms of presence and the same are linguistics and psychoanalysis. We have already seen the influence of Saussurean linguistics on Derrida's work. Many of the motifs and strategies of deconstruction are also to be found in the work of Freud and psychoanalysis.[2]

As a philosopher of memory, Freud argues that consciousness is never identical with itself. It is always inhabited by the traces of memories and traumas that resist the grasp of conscious recollection. The conscious life and identity we all take for granted is in fact the effect of an intricately woven web of conscious and unconscious traces.[3] The shock of psychoanalysis, therefore, is the challenge it poses to our traditional forms of identity and subjectivity in particular. We all like to assume that we are masters over our own conscious thoughts, but things are never that simple. Forces that resist the mastery of rational consciousness always determine our intentional thoughts, beliefs and desires. No matter how sure we are of ourselves, and what we intend to mean or say, there is always something else at work beneath the surface, as evidenced by Freud, in dreams and slips of the tongue. We can never gather the past and our sense of identity into a harmonious whole. The teleological model of memory is destined to fail.

Derrida was profoundly influenced by Freud's application of these strategies to the identity of our cultural traditions, to our understanding of the law, patriarchy and the family, and, of course, to memory and mourning. But Freud's real breakthrough, for Derrida, is his adoption of a completely new approach to analysis. In *Resistances of Psychoanalysis*, Derrida notes that the word "analysis" derives from the Greek word *analuein*, meaning to untie or to untangle. Traditional forms of analysis all presuppose this sense of analysis as the untying of threads: as the attempt to dissolve complex problems into simple elements. According to this traditional model, analysis is a process of discovery and unveiling. Faced with an initial obscurity, the analyst literally unbinds the threads of a problem, removing all resistances, allowing the truth to come to light.

This is a postal model of analysis. An original truth or meaning is deposited in a dream or a text, and it is the job of the analyst to disclose it. The task of analysis is to receive and unveil what is predestined to be discovered. A patient, for example, destines the meaning of their unconscious desires to the analyst via the medium of dreams and narratives of memory. The task of the analyst is to remove the resistances – everything that stands in the way of complete recollection – so as to reveal the truth of their desire. With Freud, however, this entire approach to analysis is transformed.

Contrary to popular opinion, psychoanalysis is not a mere art of discovery, an art of un-concealment, of bringing deep truths to the surface. Freud does not approach the unconscious of a patient as a static text awaiting the analyst to recover its true meaning. The point of analysis is never simply to say to a patient "Behold, here is the truth of your condition". Whereas the traditional model of analysis attempts to do just that, dissolving and unbinding all threads of resistance, the point of psychoanalysis is to take account of, repeat and ultimately transform these points of resistance.

Freud identifies points of resistance through the process of transference: the unconscious redirection of feelings from the patient to the analyst. This means that the task of analysis is not to take account of what the patient says but, rather, what he or she does not say. The point is to observe those points when the patient's unconscious *resists* the questioning of the analyst.

It is the moments where memory falters, where the powers of recollection run up against their own limits and impossibility, that hold the key to Freudian analysis. And it is through transference that these points of resistance come to light.

Freud's model of transference nevertheless remains within a postal economy. By means of dialogue, the patient destines the meaning of their unconscious to the analyst, who attempts to receive it. However, for Freud, like Derrida, the "true meaning" never arrives. Freud does not await the truth of a patient's unconscious desire like a letter in the post. As Derrida remarks, "Freud always maintained that resistance could not be removed by the simple discovery of the truth or by the simple revelation to the patient of the true meaning of a symptom" (R: 17). So while Freud remains within the economy of exchange between the patient and the analyst, the point of analysis is to account for the points of *resistance* that the patient transfers to the analyst; the points that *do not* offer themselves up to simple analysis.

In *The Interpretation of Dreams* (1999), for example, Freud says that every dream has a point of resistance, which he terms the "navel" or "umbilicus". The navel is the point in a dream that, like a knot or a tangle, resists all attempts at dissolution and untying; it is "the place of a tie, a knot-scar that keeps the memory of a cut and even of a severed thread at birth" (R: 11). So rather than attempting to untangle all the threads of resistance, Freud attempts to give an account of this "memory of a cut": of the points that resist all analysis and recollection.

It is not enough simply to make these points intelligible. Having identified them, the analyst then attempts to *transform* or reweave the threads of resistance: "It is all a matter of knowing how to pull threads, pull on threads, according to the art of the weaver" (R: 15). It is by means of *repetition* that Freud attempts to effect this transformation. The whole point of a therapeutic session is not simply to recollect the truth of past traumas. Having identified the points of resistance, the objective is to *repeat* and *reinterpret* these memories in a manner more conducive to the patient's mental health. And whereas the traditional model of analysis presupposes a teleological model of memory as complete recollection, for Freud the work of analysis is always incomplete. Analysis is an interminable process that attempts to help the patient come to terms with their past by encouraging them to look towards the future.

We have already seen how Derrida makes use of this model of analysis. Like Freud, Derrida never simply attempts to unveil the "true meaning" or "unconscious" of a text. Contrary to certain misrepresentations of his work, Derrida does not argue that texts possess an infinite depth or richness. This approach to analysis simply replaces a representative theory of truth – the text represents the author's intentions – with a Platonic and Hegelian model of truth – the truth of the text reveals itself from within the depths of its own unconscious resources.[4] As we saw in Chapter 2, Derrida does not believe that texts are "infinitely interpretable". To deconstruct a text is to open it up to the possibility of new readings while at the same time always respecting the fact that it is *this* particular text, with distinct themes, intentions, limits, resources and so on. In any given context, both Derrida and Freud attempt to identify and account for the structural points of *resistance* that evade the totalizing gaze of any one author, reader or analyst. The point of a deconstructive reading is to repeat and transform these points of resistance, to reweave a text in order to give it the possibility of a future. In Derrida's reading of the *Phaedrus*, for example, he remains within the economy of Plato's text while attempting to account for the points that resist its circular enclosure. Derrida identifies one such point in the figure of the *pharmakon* and, having done so, he then endeavours to repeat and transform it in an attempt to reweave Plato's text and give it new life.

In Chapter 2 we saw how repetition is always at the heart of all identity and meaning; there can be no such thing as a meaningful text without the possibility of repetition. Similarly, for Freud repetition is not just the possibility of reinterpreting past traumas in the course of a therapeutic session. What Freud calls the "repetition compulsion" is at the very heart of our psychic economies. And just as, for Derrida, repetition is inextricably tied to absence and death, so too Freud understands the repetition compulsion in terms of its relation to what he terms the "death instinct".

In *The Post Card*, Derrida traces the development of Freud's treatment of the relationship between repetition and the death instinct in *Beyond the Pleasure Principle* (1961). In this text Freud describes the libidinal economy of the unconscious in terms of two drives: the pleasure principle and the reality principle. According to Freud, the pleasure principle is the drive for pleasure, mastery and power. The reality principle is responsible for the imposition of limits that restrain the ambitions of the pleasure principle. For example, we all possess drives to violence and excess that would bring us pleasure, but the reality principle, in the form of social norms and constraints, limits and keeps the pleasure principle in check.

The relationship between these two drives follows the circular path of a postal economy. The pleasure principle passes out of itself through the reality principle in order to return to and satisfy itself. The pleasure principle destines itself to itself via the limits and obstacles imposed on it by the reality principle. According to Freud, this is a necessary detour. Derrida paraphrases Freud:

> [T]hese obstacles do sometimes prevent it from coming to its conclusion or from triumphing, but do not put it into question as

a principal tendency to pleasure, but on the contrary confirm it
as soon as they are considered as obstacles. The reality principle
imposes no definitive inhibition, no renunciation of pleasure, only
a detour in order to defer enjoyment.   (PC: 282)

According to this provisional description, the pleasure principle and the
reality principle are considered opposite terms in a postal economy. As the
original intentions of an author writing a letter must pass into its opposite
– the risks, relays and delays of the postal system – in order to return to
itself, so too the pleasure principle must pass into its opposite in order to
return to itself.

In *The Post Card*, Derrida traces the development of this economy in
Freud's text. While Derrida agrees with Freud that the pleasure principle
and the reality principle constitute a postal economy, he questions whether
we can consider them opposites. We remember that in "Plato's Pharmacy"
Derrida challenges the traditional view that speech and writing are opposites. Speech and writing also constitute a circular postal economy in which
writing is considered secondary and derivative but, as Derrida demonstrates,
the qualities that characterize writing – difference, deferral, death and repetition – also characterize the alleged purity of speech. Speech and writing are
not qualitative opposites: they are both part of the same circular movement
that is made possible by what Derrida terms archi-writing or *différance*.

Similarly, Derrida argues that, as Freud's analysis develops, the pleasure
principle and the reality principle are no longer considered opposites, but
as parts of the same movement:

[T]here is no longer any opposition, as is sometime believed,
between the pleasure principle and the reality principle. ... Because
the pleasure principle – right from this preliminary moment when
Freud grants it an uncontested mastery – enters into a contract only
with itself, reckons and speculates only with itself or with its own
metastasis, because it sends itself everything it wants, and in sum
encounters no opposition, it unleashes in itself the absolute other.
                                                            (PC: 283)

This absolute other is the point of resistance that evades the closure of the
circular economy. Freud identifies this point of resistance as repetition: "it
is repetition, precisely, that is in question here: the speculative possibility of
the totally-other (than the pleasure principle) is in advance inscribed within
it" (PC: 283). Whereas it is archi-writing that makes possible the economy
of speech and writing, it is repetition that makes possible the economy of
the pleasure principle and the reality principle.

Freud famously considers the nature of repetition by observing his grandson playing a game. His grandson had a spool attached to a thread that he would throw from his cot, and then reel back in again. As he observed this play, Freud heard the child utter *"fort"* (gone) when the spool moved away from him, and *"da"* (there) when he reeled it back. Freud speculates that the child compulsively repeats this *fort–da* game as a means to come to terms with the periodic absences of his mother. The game helps the child to articulate that while his mother may at times be gone (*"fort"*) she will always eventually return (*"da"*). It is this act of repetition, this repetition compulsion, which keeps this circular *fort–da* economy in motion.

This is yet another example of a postal economy. The child throws the spool away safe in the knowledge that it will always return (like his mother) to its rightful place. The point of Freud's example is to demonstrate that it is the repetition compulsion that drives and sustains this psychic economy. Now we have already seen in "Signature Event Context" how, as a figure of mourning, repetition is inextricably linked with death: the possibility of a text being reinterpreted in the absence of a determinate author or reader. So too for Freud the repetition compulsion is inextricably tied to the death instinct: a "death drive developed within the logic of the repetition compulsion" (PC: 363). Derrida describes how, for Freud, the postal economy of pleasure and reality is made possible only by this relation to death: "Beyond all oppositions, without any possible identification or synthesis, it is indeed a question of an economy of death" (PC: 359). And for Freud, like Derrida, the relation to death absolutely resists the all-encompassing gaze of teleological memory: "It always prevents re-appropriation from closing on itself or from achieving itself in a circle" (PC: 362). So for both thinkers repetition and death constitute the very possibility of identity, while at the same time testifying to the catastrophe of memory as the impossibility of a total and final recollection.

Although they both agree that complete recollection is impossible and that our identities are always marked by repetition and death, Derrida discerns in Freud a latent tendency to fall back on the comforting possibility of a complete and final recollection. This becomes evident in their respective approaches to the work of mourning.

In "Mourning and Melancholia" (1958), Freud describes the normal relationship we have to a loved one in terms of a postal economy. Freud refers to a person I have a relationship with as an "object of love". In a normal relationship, I invest libidinal energies in my "object of love", who dutifully returns these feelings back towards me. One might invest feelings of love in a sibling or parent, for example, who returns these feelings to me in a circular movement. All of this is thrown into disarray however, when the other – the object of love – dies. The other no longer exists to receive and return my libidinal energy, and the circle breaks. And this is what causes the feelings of grief and despair. Our normal circular relationships break down and our entire psychic economies are thrown off course.

The only way to overcome these feelings is to transfer our libidinal energies on to a new love object. In this way we can reconfigure the circular economy and get back to a normal way of functioning. So what becomes of the other when we do this? According to Freud, it is only by separating all ties to the dead other and transferring our energies on to a new love object, that we can overcome the trauma of mourning. By letting the other go in this way, we interiorize them in an *ideal* form. The concrete actual other is gone, and gone for good. But we can interiorize within ourselves an ideal form of the love object in the form of memories and recollections. In this way, we settle all accounts with the departed love object, assign it its proper place and simply get on with our lives.

This is what Freud calls a "successful" mourning. We let the actual other go, while interiorizing them in an ideal form. When this happens, the absence of the other no longer disturbs us, the work of mourning comes to completion and we simply move on to a new love object. An unsuccessful mourning is when the reconfiguration of the circular economy fails to take place. This is what Freud calls "melancholia". The melancholic cannot let the other go, and fails to interiorize it in an ideal form. In fact the melancholic interiorizes or incorporates the departed love object within itself as *still living*. Like a grieving parent who insists on keeping intact the bedroom of a deceased child, the melancholic is unable to let the actual other go. As a result, their consciousness and entire psychic economy "behaves like an open wound" (Freud 1958: 253), and they are haunted, disturbed and tormented by the dead other from which they are unable to detach themselves.

Freud's model of a successful mourning is perfectly postal and perfectly Hegelian, in that it simply negates the actual other, interiorizing (recollecting) it in an ideal form. The tears of mourning are a mere temporary detour from the proper functioning of the psychic economy. In the melancholic, however, the dead other resists this act of recollection. The dead other refuses to be exorcised and continues to haunt the psychic economy. Melancholics are incapable of simply "getting on with their lives". Even though the loved one may have departed, they have a pathological desire to keep them alive.

Derrida agrees with Freud that in mourning we have to let the other go. But he does not agree that mourning is as straightforward as Freud seems to think it is. Can we ever simply let the other go and just transfer our energies on to a new love object? Freud's description of successful (or, as he at one stage bizarrely calls it, "triumphal") mourning seems incredibly cold and mechanical if not downright oblivious to the actual experience of death. Freud writes that, "when the work of mourning is completed, the ego becomes free and uninhibited again" (1958: 245). Again, this is very Hegelian, in that death is considered a mere obstacle to be overcome in an act of interiorization and recollection. Freud goes so far as to suggest that we can "loosen the fixation" on the loved one "by disparaging it, denigrating it, and even as it were killing it" (*ibid.*: 257). Even on the death of his own daughter, Sophie, Derrida notes how Freud wrote that it was a "loss to be forgotten", that it was "as if she had never been" (PC: 329).

Is this a normal experience of mourning? Derrida does not think so. Indeed, Derrida is very sympathetic to the melancholic who is unable to let the other go. Derrida believes that we can never completely let the other go. Like the melancholic we all desire to keep the loved one close. We cannot just simply transfer our feelings on to a new "love object" and go on as if nothing has happened, as if the loved one "had never been". However, while Derrida is sympathetic to the melancholic, we cannot kid ourselves into thinking that the other is actually still living within us. In *Mémoires: For Paul de Man*, Derrida writes:

> For never will we believe either in death or immortality; and we sustain the blaze of this terrible light through devotion, for it would be unfaithful to delude oneself into believing that the other living in us is living in himself: because he lives in us and because we live this or that in his memory, in memory of him. This being "in us," the being "in us" of the other, in bereaved memory, can be neither the so-called resurrection of the other himself (the other is dead and nothing can save him from this death, nor can anyone save us from it), nor the simple inclusion of a narcissistic fantasy in a subjectivity that is closed upon itself or even identical to itself. (MdP: 21–2)

Derrida argues that a successful mourning (in Freud's sense) would fail as a work of mourning, as it fails to respect the singularity of the other and allow them a future. Conversely, a failed mourning (in Freud's sense) would "succeed" for Derrida, as it would keep the actual other close, respecting the fact that they resist all our attempts to assign them their proper and final resting place:

> We can only live this experience in the form of an aporia: the aporia of mourning and of prosopopeia, where the possible remains impossible. Where success fails. And where faithful interiorization bears the other and constitutes him in me (in us), at once living and dead. It makes the other a part of us, between us – and then the other no longer quite seems to be the other, because we grieve

for him and bear him in us, like an unborn child, like a future. And inversely, the failure succeeds: an aborted interiorization is at the same time a respect for the other as other, a sort of tender rejection, a movement of renunciation which leaves the other alone, outside, over there, in his death, outside of us. (MdP: 35)

Freud's model of "successful" mourning fails to respect our deep need to keep the departed with us. For Derrida, the work of mourning desires both that success fails and that failure succeeds. We want the act of mourning to be interminable because in this way we can be faithful to the other and keep them with us.[5] But while Derrida and the melancholic desire to keep the ghosts of memory alive, the scientific Freud, the Freud of enlightenment reason and scientific protocol, wants to exorcise his theories of all such spectral traces. While Derrida admires the Freud who thinks the catastrophe of memory in terms of repetition and death, according to *this* Freud, the melancholic is a clinical aberration, a problem who has to be dealt with and "cured" of the ailment. Freud is a thinker of resistance and loss, but his model of successful mourning betrays the more scientific Freud, who secretly desires to assign everything its proper place within a comprehensive scientific explanation. Like all self-respecting scientists, Freud does not believe in ghosts. But Derrida consistently warns of the nostalgia that tempts us to think that we can ever be done with the past, that we can just assign it its proper place and move on. Despite all his protestations to the contrary, Freud's scientific ambitions will always be incomplete. He can never completely exorcise the melancholic traces of mourning and loss. It is precisely this tension between, on the one hand, the Freud of catastrophe and loss, and on the other, the Freud of science and recollection, that fascinates Derrida; and he discerns a similar tension in the works of Husserl and Heidegger.

Husserl and phenomenology

The father of modern phenomenology is the Moravian-born philosopher Edmund Husserl. The term "phenomenology" comes from the Greek words *phenomenon* and *logos*. Phenomenology is literally the science, discourse or description (*logos*) of things as they appear or show themselves to us (*phenomenon*). Husserl developed the phenomenological method in response to the problem of scepticism in modern epistemology. Epistemology is the theory of knowledge: the theory of how we acquire and validate our knowledge. The problem of modernist epistemology arose with the separation, by the French philosopher René Descartes, of the world into two distinct substances: mind (*res cogitans*) and matter (*res extensa*). The problem then became how to bridge the gap between these two substances. How does an immaterial mind interact with a material world? How is knowledge as a result of this interaction possible? Is our knowledge founded on immaterial innate ideas, or is it derived from experience? How can we ever be sure that the knowledge we have of the world actually corresponds to the world as it really is?

To this day, philosophers are still debating these questions, with some arguing that the foundation of all knowledge is in the mind (rationalists) and others arguing that all knowledge is founded in experience (empiricists). According to Husserl, however, the problem of scepticism – of how we can ever be certain about the validity of our knowledge – is irreducible, due to the very conceptual framework that Descartes bequeathed to the philosophical tradition. The only way we can overcome the problem of scepticism is by completely rethinking our view of the world in terms of an opposition between mind and matter, subject and object.

According to Husserl, Descartes's mistake was in simply assuming the "givenness" of the subject–object relation. Descartes assumes the presence or givenness of a knowing subject and the presence or givenness of an object. The problem for Descartes then is how to bridge the gap between the two. For Husserl, however, we do not originally experience the world as self-present conscious subjects encountering self-present objects. The very subject–object relation that Descartes takes for granted as his starting-point is, for Husserl, a secondary abstraction from a more originary experience of the world.

In our originary experience of the world, consciousness is always consciousness-*of* something. Consciousness does not exist apart from its relation to the world: they are always interwoven with each other (Husserl uses the term "intentionality" to describe this more originary relation). The understanding of consciousness as something distinct and detached from the world only happens later. The task of phenomenology is to shake loose the constraints of the Cartesian model, and to reawaken and describe this more originary experience.

Many of Derrida's neologisms and deconstructive strategies are foreshadowed in Husserl's theory of intentionality. Derrida's arguments that speech is always inhabited by writing, that the inside is always contaminated by the outside and so on, are direct descendants of Husserl's claim that subject and object are not simple opposites, but originally interwoven with each other. Indeed, the single most important factor that distinguishes Derrida from the structuralist school of thought that became so popular in Europe and the United States in the 1960s, was the fact that he read Saussure in the context of phenomenological questions that he inherited from Husserl. Derrida's first three books were closely detailed readings of Husserl, in particular Husserl's engagement with the question of ideality (the necessity of the "all or nothing"). In his introduction to Husserl's *Origin of Geometry*, for example, Derrida engages in a detailed reading of Husserl's account of the possibility of the ideality or "truth" of mathematical objects; a fact that is often ignored by all those who accuse Derrida of renouncing the value of truth altogether.[6]

Although Husserl was a formative influence on Derrida's early work, Derrida discerns in his phenomenology a nostalgic desire for recollection and completion. Like Freud, Husserl is both a thinker of repetition and the catastrophe of memory, while at the same time harbouring a secret desire to account for everything within an all embracing scientific theory. But before we get to that, let us examine how repetition and the impossibility of recollection play a central role in Husserl's phenomenology.

If our experience of the world is always the result of intentional activity, of the fact that consciousness is always consciousness-of something, then this activity is always postal. Our experience of the world is the result of an intentional activity, which projects an anticipatory horizon – an initial interpretation of the world – which it subsequently confirms or rejects. Take the familiar experience of mistaking someone on the street. If I am walking down the street and I see someone approaching whom I take to be my friend John, then this person appears to me within an interpretative horizon. But if, as I get closer, I come to realize that this is not in fact my friend but a stranger, then my initial interpretative horizon is rejected and replaced by another. Intentional activity therefore is postal in that it destines a particular interpretation of the world for itself, which it either duly receives or rejects and returns to sender.

Now what this means for Husserl, is that our experience of the world is never simply given: it is never simply present (as Descartes claims) before us. Our experience is always the result of interpretation and *repetition*: the constant confirmation and denial of our interpretative horizons. So the identity of the individual who appears before me on the street is always provisional. It is always possible that at any given moment my intentions will be unfulfilled, compelling me to project a new horizon. So for Husserl, like Derrida and Freud, repetition is not the mere reproduction of the same. Repetition is at the very heart of identity; it is what constitutes identity and makes it possible.[7]

If our intentional activity is postal, however, and follows a circular movement of destining and receiving, then the circle is always cut. Like Freud, Husserl believes that something always resists and evades our attempts to close the circle. We never recollect our identities in their pure form.

Intentional activity is always interpretative, which means that our experience of the world is always partial and incomplete. When I perceive an object, for example, I can only perceive it from a particular perspective. I can walk around it and perceive it from different angles, but at any given moment there will always be something that resists my gaze. Its identity will always be the effect of the repetition of intentional acts. And if I perceive my friend John, not only will my perceptions of him be determined according to my limited perspective, but his conscious thoughts, the inner workings of his mind, will always evade my attempts to have a complete and perfect knowledge of him.

The objects of our experience, therefore, never simply present themselves to us. Something always resists any one particular perspective. At any given moment, the presence or identity of an object is always incomplete; it is always marked by the traces of absence, loss and death. And these traces play a *constitutive* role in the formation of identity. The very possibility of identity, we remember, is the impossibility of completion and recollection. It is only on the basis of incompletion and loss that we can experience the world at all. Indeed, in *Ideas I* (1983), Husserl goes so far as to posit the notion of the possible annihilation of the world; that at any given moment the world as we know it could possibly erupt into chaos. Husserl's point is that our experience of the world always contains within itself this possibility of death and annihilation; a possibility that plays a constitutive role in our lived experience.[8] So like Freud, Husserl's theory of intentionality accounts for the fact that our lived experience is haunted by the spectral traces of absence and loss, repetition and death.

Husserl too was a man of science who had no time for ghosts and spectres, and who strived to exorcise the traces of mourning and loss from his conception of philosophy as rigorous science. Husserl's overall project belongs to the tradition that conceives the task of philosophy as providing an indubitable foundation for the sciences. Like many of the thinkers of the late-nineteenth and early-twentieth centuries, Husserl desires to give an accurate scientific description of the ideal structures of human experience that would transcend the partial experiences of any one particular individual. In the same way that Frege attempts to deduce the ideal objective laws of logic independent of individual human psychology, so too Husserl attempts to describe the ideal contents of transcendental consciousness independent of the historical contingent existence of particular conscious individuals. Like Frege and Russell, Husserl desires to separate the necessary from the contingent, the essential from the accidental.

One way that Husserl attempts to achieve this separation is by means of the phenomenological reduction or *epoché*, whereby our every day existence – what Husserl calls the "natural attitude" – is bracketed out of the domain of pure phenomenological description. It is only by extricating ourselves from the concrete reality of contingency and the accidental that we can truly acquire a scientific knowledge of things as they really are. So whereas the natural attitude is the realm of contingency, loss and death, the point of the reduction is to disclose the realm of pure transcendental life in which "death is recognized as but an empirical and extrinsic signification, a worldly accident" (SP: 10). While the hermeneutic Husserl thinks the catastrophe of memory as the impossibility of complete recollection, the Husserl of first philosophy and phenomenological science thinks the *epochē*, freed from the limits of contingency and death, as the possibility of the complete recollection or intuition of the pure essence of things.

In *Speech and Phenomena* Derrida problematizes Husserl's attempt to separate the essential from the accidental by means of a sustained critique of the latter's theory of signification as outlined in his *Logical Investigations* (2001). In this influential text, Husserl attempts to describe a pure logical grammar that would separate the pure ideal meanings of thought from the impure contingency of natural languages. Derrida argues that Husserl's attempt to do so, indeed the entire phenomenological project itself, rests on a particular distinction that Husserl attempts to enforce between two types of signification.

In the first of his investigations in the chapter entitled "Expression and Meaning", Husserl makes a distinction between two types of sign. According to Husserl, "every sign is a sign for something, but not every sign has 'meaning,' a 'sense' that the sign expresses" (Husserl 2001: 103). Husserl distinguishes between two types of sign: the expressive and the indicative. An indicative sign is a sign that, while it does signify, does not carry within it an intention to mean *per se*. For example, gathering clouds may be a sign of impending rain, but the clouds merely indicate this possibility. According to Husserl, we are motivated to associate rain with the gathering clouds, but we would not say that the clouds mean to signify rain.

An expressive sign, however, does contain a genuine meaning in the sense of an animating intention that literally means to say something (the French term for meaning, *vouloir dire* – literally "wanting to say" – captures this sense of "meaning"). Expressive signs contain within themselves the animating breath of a living intention. Indicative signs, in contrast, are lifeless, empty material signifiers that merely refer to one another by means of association. Expression is the medium of pure, self-present living intentions, while indication – which always requires the materiality of the sign – is the medium of difference, deferral, repetition and death. So in order to fulfil his goal of describing the pure ideality of meanings prior to their contamination by natural languages, it is imperative for Husserl to make a sharp distinction between expressive and indicative discourse.

Now, an expressive sign can take on an indicative function. The only way we can communicate our expressions is through recourse to indicative signs. The risk here, of course, is that in allowing our pure intentions to literally "fall into the world" in an indicative sign (natural language) we can no longer safeguard their original meaning. In becoming contaminated with indication, the original expressive intention always runs the risk of being misinterpreted and abused. So Husserl has inherited the Platonic problem of how to purify the living presence of an original expression from the errancy and death of signification.

Husserl, therefore, not only rules out indication as a means to the pure ideality of meaning, he also calls for the decontamination of expressive intentions of signification altogether. And given that the attempt to communicate our expressions runs the risk of contamination, Husserl follows Plato in focusing his analysis on the expressive intent of the living voice, which Husserl equates with the interior monologue of consciousness in communion with itself. As Derrida remarks, "we have to ferret out the unshaken purity of expression in a language without communication, in speech as monologue, in the completely muted voice of the 'solitary mental life'" (SP: 22).

Once again, however, repetition plays a crucial role in Derrida's analysis. While Husserl wants to exclude all repetition as indication from expression, an expressive act still has to present itself as such (it is only recognizable through being repeated). Husserl therefore has to distinguish between the "real" repetition of indicative communication and the "imaginary" representation of pure interior monologue. Derrida writes:

> The reduction to the monologue is really a putting of empirical worldly existence between brackets. In "solitary mental life" we no longer use real (*wirklich*) words, but only imagined (*vorgestellt*) words. And lived experience – about which we were wondering whether it might not be "indicated" to the speaking subject by himself – does not have to be so indicated because it is immediately certain and present to itself. While in real communication existing signs *indicate* other existences, which are only probable and mediately evoked, in the monologue when the expression is *full*, non-existent signs *show* significations (*Bedeutungen*) that are ideal (and thus non-existent) and certain (for they are presented to intuition). The certitude of inner existence, Husserl thinks, has no need to be signified. It is immediately present to itself. It is living consciousness.
>
> (SP: 43)

Husserl attempts to make a qualitative distinction between expression as representation (*Vorstellung*) and indication as repetition (*Vergegenwärtigung*).

While the latter is qualified as the difference, deferral and death characteristic of all forms of signification, the former is conceived as an inner monologue in which consciousness speaks to itself without any need of signification. Inner monologue hears and comprehends itself ("*je m'entende*") as soon as it speaks: "My words are 'alive' because they seem not to leave me: not to fall outside me, outside my breath, at a visible distance" (SP: 76). According to Husserl, inner monologue does not communicate to itself in the way that indicative language communicates. While the latter relies on signs that are external to it, the former comprehends itself in "absolute proximity" to itself. Living solitary consciousness recollects everything to itself without the risks of signification and loss.

> When I speak, it belongs to the phenomenological essence of this operation that I hear myself [*je m'entende*] at the same time that I speak. The signifier, animated by my breath and the meaning-intention … is in absolute proximity to me. The living act, the life-giving act, the *Lebendigkeit*, which animates the body of the signifier and transforms it into meaningful expression, the soul of language seems not to separate itself from itself, from its own self-presence. It does not risk death in the body of a signifier that is given over to the world and the visibility of space. (SP: 77–8)

While the repetition of indication (*Vergegenwärtigung*) relies on signs that function in the absence of an original meaning-intention, and always risks the possibility of misinterpretation and loss, the representation of expression (*Vorstellung*) has no need of signs: it does not risk death. The question for Derrida is whether or not Husserl can maintain this qualitative distinction: whether or not Husserl can, in fact, decontaminate expression and consciousness of all indication and signification.

In his attempt to do so, Husserl appeals to the fact that in inner monologue consciousness communicates with itself in the pure presence of the "now". But, as Derrida points out, Husserl himself challenges this very conception of the "now" in terms of presence. In his work on internal time consciousness, Husserl argues that the "now" moment is in fact the effect of a play of retentional and protentional traces. There is never a simple "now" point. Like the elements of meaning for Saussure, the "now" of presence is always determined in relation to a no-longer-present of the past (retention) and a not-yet-present of the future (protention). Our experience of presence and the "now" is always the effect of this temporal weave. This means that the "now" is always incomplete. It is always marked by the traces of absence: of the past that is no longer and the future that is yet to come.

In order to overcome this dilemma, Husserl again follows Plato in attempting to distinguish between "primary" memory (retention) and "secondary" memory (reproduction). To illustrate what he means by primary memory, Husserl appeals to the example of a musical melody. When we listen to a series of musical notes we do not hear them as disjointed and independent sounds. We always hear the notes of a melody "all at once", as a unified now-moment. As the different notes are sounded, we retain the notes that have just been heard by means of an act of retention or primary memory. Husserl distinguishes this from reproduction or secondary memory. While retention retains a sounded note in the lived presence of the "now", reproduction merely recalls a past memory that is no longer present (a melody we may have heard earlier in a performance, for example). So, like Plato, Husserl attempts to make a qualitative distinction between a primary memory (*mnesis*), which retains a living presence, and a secondary memory (*hypomnesis*), which merely repeats past events in their absence.

As Derrida argues, however, Husserl cannot maintain this distinction; he cannot safeguard the pure presence of the "now" from absence and loss. Derrida asks what it could possibly mean to try to make a qualitative distinction between a moment that has just lapsed, and a moment that has been lapsed for some time. The key word here is *qualitative*. Husserl claims that our two lapsed moments are qualitatively different, that they are different in kind or in principle. But as Derrida argues, a moment cannot be just a little bit lapsed. A moment is lapsed whether it has just happened or whether it happened hours ago. Retention and reproduction are not qualitatively but *quantitatively* different. Their difference is determined not as a difference in kind, but according to their relative distance from the now-point that they share in common. Retention and reproduction are both examples of representation in general, which means that *both* of them function in the absence of an original presence; *both* of them are marked by the traces of absence and loss:

> The difference between retention and reproduction, between primary and secondary memory, is not the radical difference Husserl wanted between perception and nonperception; it is rather a difference between two modifications of nonperception. … Once again, this relation to nonpresence neither befalls, surrounds, nor conceals the presence of the primordial impression; rather it makes possible its ever renewed upsurge and virginity.   (SP: 66–7)

Of course the retention–reproduction distinction is just another version of the distinction between repetition as *Vorstellung* and repetition as *Vergegenwärtigung*. And just as the absence that characterizes reproduction is also at the heart of retention, so too the difference, deferral and death that characterize indication and signification are at the heart of expression and the inner life of silent monologue. Despite Husserl's attempts to exclude them from living consciousness, repetition and signification precede identity and expression and make them possible: "We thus come – against Husserl's express intention – to make the *Vorstellung* itself, and as such, depend on the possibility of re-presentation (*Vergegenwärtigung*). The presence-of-the-present is derived from repetition and not the reverse" (SP: 52).

Husserl cannot succeed in his attempt to separate the necessary from the contingent, expression and presence from indication and signification. Contrary to his claims, signs are always inside the "now" and solitary consciousness; we could not even conceive of the latter without the former. Husserl cannot exorcise his analysis of signification and death. Derrida writes:

> The relationship with my death (my disappearance in general) thus lurks in this determination of being as presence, ideality, the absolute possibility of repetition. The possibility of the sign is this relationship with death. The determination and elimination of the sign in metaphysics is the dissimulation of this relationship with death, which yet produced signification. (SP: 54)

Like Freud, therefore, Husserl is a thinker of the catastrophe of memory and the impossibility of completely recollecting our identities. But again like Freud, Husserl also strives to account for everything in an all-encompassing scientific description. Just as Freud's model of successful mourning attempts to separate the ideal form of the departed loved one from their incarnate existence, so too Husserl attempts to separate the ideality of meanings from their incarnation in natural languages and indicative discourse. There can be no time for mourning in Husserl. Death is a mere obstacle to be overcome and assigned its proper place within the greater project of a pure phenomenological science. Despite all his efforts, however, Husserl cannot immunize the alleged purity of consciousness from signification, repetition and death. To understand more about the relationship between phenomenology and death we turn now to Husserl's infamous student Martin Heidegger.

Martin Heidegger

In *The Post Card*, Derrida argues that the other great master-thinker of the post is Heidegger:

> Here Freud and Heidegger, I conjoin them within me like two great ghosts of the "great epoch." The two surviving grandfathers. They did not know each other, but according to me they form a couple, and in fact just because of that, this singular anachrony. They are bound to each other without reading each other and without corresponding. (PC: 191)

It is fair to say that while both Freud and Husserl have had a considerable influence on Derrida, his deconstructive project would be literally unthinkable without the enormous influence of Heidegger. In conversation with Richard Kearney, Derrida remarks:

> My philosophical formation owes much to the thought of Husserl, Heidegger and Hegel. Heidegger is probably the most constant influence, and particularly his project of overcoming/deconstructing Greek metaphysics. Husserl, whom I studied in a more detailed and painstaking fashion, taught me a certain methodical prudence and reserve, a rigorous technique of unraveling and formulating questions. But I never shared Husserl's pathos for, and commitment to, a phenomenology of presence. In fact, it was Husserl's method that helped me to suspect the very notion of presence and the fundamental role it played in all philosophies. My relationship with Heidegger is much more enigmatic and extensive: here my interest was not just methodological but existential. The content and themes of Heidegger's questioning excited me – especially the "ontological difference," the critique of Platonism and the relationship between language and Being. (DO: 141)

The term "deconstruction" is an attempt to reinterpret Heidegger's German term *Abbau*, and many of Derrida's deconstructive neologisms – the trace, the double-bind, *différance*, cinders and so on – have their origin in his critical engagement with the work of Heidegger. But as with his relationship to Freud and Husserl, Derrida's relationship to Heidegger is far from simple. While his influence is an integral part of his work, Derrida always insists on maintaining a critical distance from Heidegger: "I believe, in numerous ways, what I write does not, shall we say *resemble* a text of Heideggerian filiation ... I have marked quite explicitly, in *all* the essays I have published, as can be verified, a *departure* from the Heideggerian problematic" (Pos: 54). We shall return below to Derrida's reasons for this "departure". For the moment let us take a look at some of the important contributions of Heidegger's thought to twentieth-century philosophy and Derrida in particular.[9]

Heidegger was born in Messkirch in southern Germany in 1889. After spending some time in a Jesuit seminary, the young Heidegger moved to the University of Freiburg, where he eventually became an assistant to Husserl. It was Husserl's phenomenological method that ignited Heidegger's philosophical imagination and continued to have a lasting influence on his work.

As a student of Husserl's, Heidegger attempted to take phenomenology in new and exciting directions. Heidegger shifts Husserl's radical breakthrough from epistemology (the question of knowledge) to ontology (the question of Being). Whereas for Husserl, the key word is "consciousness", for Heidegger it is "Being". So rather than describing man's experience in terms of intentional structures of consciousness, Heidegger re-describes man's experience in terms of existential structures of being-in-the-world. Heidegger argues that Husserl's theory of intentionality is itself a secondary effect of a more primordial relation: an originary understanding of Being.

According to Heidegger, the question of Being has been forgotten in the Western philosophical tradition. Heidegger does not suggest that Being has never been a topic of discussion and debate in Western philosophy; the tradition is replete with metaphysical theories of Being stretching from Plato and Aristotle, through Aquinas, Hegel and beyond. Heidegger, however, argues that how we think about Being has always been taken for granted. We have forgotten the question of Being precisely as a *question*. We have inherited a very specific understanding of Being from the ancient Greeks, which we have failed to question ever since. The point of phenomenology, for Heidegger, is to reopen this question.

We all have what Heidegger calls a pre-comprehension of the meaning of Being. Our very use of the verb "to be" implies that we all have some awareness of what we mean when we say something like "This *is* a book about Jacques Derrida." According to Heidegger, our pre-comprehension of the meaning of Being has always interpreted Being in terms of *presence*. We all assume an understanding of the Being of an entity (this book for example) as its simply being-present here before us. The issue of the nature of its Being then becomes an issue of its "whatness", its "essence": "What is the essence of this entity that presents itself here before me?" This understanding is exemplified for Heidegger in the scientific attitude that always attempts to understand what something is by getting to grips with its internal "essence", with the sheer "whatness" of a thing.

Heidegger wants to shift this approach to the question of Being in terms of the "whatness" of an entity to an interrogation of the "howness" of an entity. The question Heidegger asks is: "Why is there something rather than nothing?" How is it that an entity can present itself to us in the first place? How is it that there *is* a world at all for us to experience? Heidegger wants to shift the question of Being from an enquiry into the "whatness" of the world, which is present before us, to an interrogation of *how* the world presents itself to us at all. How is our experience of Being possible?

In attempting to answer this question, Heidegger follows Husserl's conviction that the dualism between subject (the self) and object (the world beyond self – the "external" world) was misguided and mistaken. Heidegger argues that it was Descartes's contention that the thinking self (*cogito*) could doubt away its environment in an effort to establish its own certainty, which was primarily responsible for concretizing the subject–object divide. But according to Heidegger, even Husserl fell into the trap of this dualism. Husserl's emphasis on the role of intentional consciousness in the formation of the self's constitution was seen by Heidegger to be yet another unfortunate consequence of the Cartesian legacy, even if Husserl's original aim was to surmount the subject–object divide by leading us back to an originary experience of the world. For Heidegger there is no way the subject can, or should, try to extricate itself from the world in which it finds itself. For it is through our basic *interaction* with the world that we come to a genuine and fundamental understanding of the "how" of Being.

The question of Being, the question that first stimulated the early Greek metaphysicians, is thus what Heidegger intends to retrieve. He does so by underscoring our being-there (*Da-sein*), our temporal situatedness *in* the world, as distinct from our consciousness *of* the world. Due to the fact that a human being is the only being capable of asking the question "What does it mean to be?", any examination of being must therefore proceed by way of an enquiry into the human self as a being-there (*Dasein*): as a being who is concretely submerged in the practical affairs of the everyday world.

One such way that Heidegger approaches the question of the Being of *Dasein* is through an analysis of the category of "understanding". Like Husserl, Heidegger wants to make explicit the interpretative horizons that structure our experience. But *contra* Husserl, "understanding" does not denote conscious awareness or assimilation. According to Heidegger, we exist before we are objectively aware that we exist; our existence is *pre-understanding*, in the sense that we pre-reflectively interpret the world as a project of possibilities for our existence, before coming to reflectively understand it as such. Whereas for Husserl the interpretative horizons of intentional consciousness might determine an object as a hammer, and then proceed to intuit or recollect its essence or "whatness", for Heidegger our understanding projects an interpretative horizon in which the same object appears as a *tool* for hammering, as a means to fulfil certain projects that *Dasein* has projected for itself.

To understand is not to understand facts, but to understand what possibilities are open to us in the situation in which we find ourselves. As such, human existence constitutes what Heidegger famously calls a "hermeneutic circle", which means it implicitly interprets itself in terms of its everyday moods and projects before it raises this interpretation to the level of philosophical speculation. Hermeneutic understanding reveals things (such as hammers) in terms of their possible serviceability for me, and it does so by releasing them from the abstraction of a timeless present (their "whatness") into the temporal horizons of my concrete concerns: retrieving the meaningfulness of these entities from my past experience or projecting such meaningfulness into my future possible experiences.

Now there is postal economy at work here. *Dasein* projects an understanding of the world, in which it then discovers entities to help it realize the projects it has projected for itself. Take the familiar experience of buying a new car, a green BMW, for example. While you never noticed them before, now everywhere you go you see green BMWs. The reason for this is that, having purchased this particular car, you have projected a new horizon, a new form of understanding, in which green BMWs now matter for you. Of course, the same green BMWs existed prior to your purchase, but they simply did not appear within the horizon of your world. Having projected an understanding of the world in which green BMWs *are* a matter of concern for you, you now discover them everywhere. They literally show themselves to you in a way that they did not before. This is a postal economy. *Dasein* projects (destines/sends) an understanding of the world, which it then receives and re-discovers. The car owner discovers an understanding of the world that she herself has projected onto it.

Like Freud and Husserl, however, the circle of Heidegger's postal economy is always cut; it never comes to completion. *Dasein* is never complete and present to itself. Its essence is its *existence*, which means that *Dasein* is literally "outside itself", continually projecting new projects and possibilities. The hermeneutic circle never comes to rest, but keeps on turning and turning. This is why for Heidegger, like Freud and Husserl, the hermeneutic circle is an effect of *repetition*. Whereas for Husserl our identities are always the effect of repetition as the constant confirmation and denial of intentional acts, the identity of *Dasein* is an effect of its being continually in the process of inheriting and projecting new possibilities for itself. As long as *Dasein* is alive, it is never complete. It is only on the event of its death that the circle comes to rest.

This is why from the moment that we are born we are already a being-towards-death. Death is not a mere end, the mere cessation of life. We project ourselves towards the future precisely *because* we are going to die. Death is not one event like any other that just happens to occur at the end of one's life. On the contrary, death is imminent in our every waking moment. It is because we can die at any moment that we desire to live at all. So as in Freud and Husserl, it is repetition and death that drive the hermeneutic circle and prevent it from closing in on itself; and this is why Heidegger argues that death is *Dasein's* most "proper possibility".

The whole point of Heidegger's existential analysis, however, is to give a complete description of the being of *Dasein*. If *Dasein* only comes to completion on the event of its death, then how can we testify to this moment of completion? How can we testify to our own deaths? Of course this is impossible, because at the moment of my death, I cease to exist. *Dasein* will always be too early and too late. Death may be *Dasein's* most proper possibility, but death itself is an impossibility for *Dasein*. But while death itself may resist all phenomenological description, Heidegger believes that we nonetheless have to give an account of it.

In *Aporias*, Derrida analyses Heidegger's account of death as *Dasein's* most "proper possibility" in *Being and Time* (1962). At one point in his reading, Derrida writes: "At stake for me here is approaching a certain enigmatic relation among dying, testifying, and surviving" (A: 30). Derrida is interested in how Heidegger thinks dying, how he can give an account of, or testify to it, and what if anything survives or resists his conception of death.

In *Being and Time*, Heidegger attempts to distinguish the existential analysis of death from the conceptions of death common to both metaphysics and biology. We all have a certain conception of death. Culturally and scientifically, we all have an understanding of what we mean when we talk about death. According to Heidegger, however, all of these conceptions presuppose an ontological pre-understanding of death. His aim in *Being and Time* is to make this pre-understanding explicit.

In order to do this, Heidegger has first to distinguish this pre-understanding of death from two other conceptions of what it means to die: perishing (*Verenden*) and demise (*Ableben*). By perishing, Heidegger simply means the ending of the living: the coming to the end that all living things share. By demise, Heidegger means passing away, literally leaving life, and crossing the threshold of death. Now to both of these conceptions of death, Heidegger opposes "properly dying".

Only *Dasein* can die properly, because only *Dasein* has an understanding of its death as a possibility. Only *Dasein* can relate to the possibility of its death *as such*. All this means is that we are fully aware (although we spend most of our time trying to avoid this awareness) that we are going to die. Animals, for example, (according to Heidegger) have no conception of their deaths as an actual possibility. Animals eat and avoid predators but this is because of evolutionary instincts rather than any kind of conception of the actual possibility of their deaths. So as *Dasein* relates to the hammer always *as* a tool to realize a particular possibility, so too *Dasein* relates to its own death *as* its most proper possibility.

The question then becomes: "How does *Dasein* testify to its own death?" Is not death the cessation of all testimony? How can the cessation of all possibility be at the same time *Dasein*'s most proper possibility? In answer to these questions Derrida argues that in Heidegger's text "it is therefore necessary to isolate two typical series of ontological statements concerning possibility" (A: 63–4).

The first statements are assertions that characterize death as *Dasein*'s most proper possibility, as we have already seen. The very essence of *Dasein* is its "being-possible" and death is the most proper possibility of this possibility. As Derrida writes:

> This possibility of being is not a simple characteristic to be noted or described. In its essential and constant imminence, it must be *assumed*; one can and one must testify to it; and the testimony is not a mere constative report: the statements of the existential analysis are originarily prescriptive or normative. (A: 64)

Dasein must testify to its death. In *Being and Time* Heidegger writes: "Death is a possibility-of-being that Dasein itself has to take over in every case. With death, Dasein awaits itself in its ownmost potentiality-for-being" (Heidegger 1962: 250; quoted in A: 64). This is just a complicated way of saying that we can only begin to live our lives when we accept the inevitability of our own deaths. Our being is always a being-towards-death. And in this sense even death is postal. In the midst of its existence *Dasein* destines its death to itself as its most proper possibility.

The second series of statements involve what Derrida terms an "aporetic supplement" of *impossibility* to possibility: "Insofar as it is its most proper possibility, and precisely as such, death is also for Dasein, Heidegger ultimately says, the possibility of an impossibility" (A: 68). To experience my own death is an impossibility. So what can Heidegger mean by this possibility of impossibility?

This is the point at which Derrida and Heidegger start to part company. Derrida also speaks about impossibility, but for Derrida the impossible can never be reduced to a form of possibility. To do so would be to draw the impossible back into a traditional circular economy organized around a form of presence. For Heidegger on the other hand, the impossibility of testifying to my death *is* a possibility that *Dasein* can testify to as such. While death is impossible *per se* for *Dasein*, we nonetheless can think this impossibility within the radar of the possible.

> Heidegger would thus say that for Dasein impossibility as death
> – the impossibility of death, the impossibility of the existence whose

name is "death" – can appear as such and announce itself; it can make itself awaited or let itself be awaited as possible and as such.

(A: 74)

While the experience of death is impossible for *Dasein*, *Dasein* can still testify to this impossibility, in that it can testify to it *as* an impossibility. So death has its proper place for Heidegger. Death *is* that which is impossible for *Dasein*.

Derrida argues, however, that death and the impossible resist *absolutely* all reduction to possibility. The impossible is that which always survives and resists any testimony. Derrida writes that he wishes to explore the relationship between dying, testimony and survival in Heidegger's analysis. But while Derrida and Heidegger both share a conception of our relation to death as that which resists all enclosure within a circular economy, and while both agree that we have to give an account of and testify to this relation, Derrida distances himself from Heidegger's attempt to think the impossibility of this relation *as* a possibility.

For all they share in common, Derrida consistently discerns a latent nostalgia for presence and possibility in Heidegger's work. According to Derrida, Heidegger never quite shook off the shackles of the tradition that he so expertly diagnosed in the work of others. Whereas Derrida thinks death and the impossible in terms of spectral traces and the absolute impossibility of recollection, Heidegger draws closer to Freud in thinking death in terms of the proper, assigning it its proper place within a fundamental ontology. While Heidegger does not share the scientific predispositions of his predecessors, there is ultimately no mourning in his philosophy. There are no ghosts, no spectral remains, that resist Heidegger's attempts to gather everything in terms of the meaning and truth of Being.

In his later work Heidegger attempted to move beyond what he felt to be too anthropological an approach to the question of Being. In these writings Heidegger no longer engages the question of Being in terms of the meaning of the being of *Dasein*; rather, he attunes himself to the "truth" or "event" of Being as it reveals itself in the history of Western metaphysics. For the later Heidegger, the history of philosophy is the history of Being itself as it announces itself through the works of selected thinkers.

Ever since Plato and the great Greek metaphysicians stamped the seal of presence on our understanding of Being, the great mystery and wonder of Being, the sheer appreciation of the strangeness of things, has been forgotten. For the later Heidegger, Being still manages to give or send itself to us by means of language. But while the mainstream tradition has completely deafened itself to the wonder and strangeness of the truth of Being, we can still hear its mystery in the works of certain thinkers and poets who have managed to attune themselves to the mystery of Being's call.

This again is a postal economy. The truth of Being gives or destines itself (the English "there is" is translated into German as "*es gibt*" – literally "it gives"), by means of language, to be received and thought by man. Heidegger once famously remarked that "we are too late for the gods, and too early for Being" (1971: 4). The original experience of the mystery of Being, which was allegedly known to the early Greeks, has been forgotten in the philosophical tradition. The task of philosophy and of thinking in general is to attune itself to the call of Being: to await the message that Being has specially destined for us.

According to Derrida, however, the later Heidegger falls into the same trap as the Heidegger of *Being and Time*. While Derrida consistently emphasizes impossibility, dis-adjustment and incompletion, he discerns in Heidegger an attempt to do the opposite: "one of the recurrent critiques or deconstructive questions that I pose to Heidegger has to do with the privilege Heidegger grants to what he calls *Versammlung*, gathering, which is always more powerful than dissociation. I would say exactly the opposite" (VR: 14).

Derrida thinks the catastrophe of memory, the impossibility of complete recollection, as a work of mourning. When we mourn we desire both to keep/gather *and* let go, and it is this sense of loss and letting go that keeps the work of mourning alive. But there is no such sense of loss in Heidegger. If Derrida is a thinker of loss and mourning, then Heidegger is ultimately a thinker of gathering (*Versammlung*) and adjustment (*Dike*). In *Mémoires: For Paul de Man*, Derrida notes how, in *What is called Thinking?* (1968), Heidegger meditates on the common root of the words "thought" (*Gedachtes*) and "memory" (*Gedächtnis*). According to Heidegger both of these terms have their origin in the German word "*Gedanc*". Derrida quotes Heidegger:

> What does thinking mean here? Is memory no more than a container for the thought of thinking or does thinking itself rest in memory? ... Let us address our question now to the history of words. It gives us a direction, though the historical representation of this history is still incomplete and will presumably always remain so. We hear the hint, echoing in the spoken aspect of the aforementioned words, that the decisive and originally speaking word is: the "Gedanc." But "Gedanc" does not mean, when all is said and done, what we currently mean when we today use the word "thought" (*Gedanke*). A thought usually means: an idea, a presentation, an opinion, an inspiration. The originary word "Gedanc" says: the gathered, all-gathering recollection.   (Quoted in MdP: 92)

Heidegger goes on to argue that: "The '*Gedanc*,' the bottom of the heart, is the gathering together (*versammlung*) of all that concerns us, all that comes to us, all that touches us insofar as we are, as human beings" (quoted in MdP: 92–3). The thought of Being, therefore, is an act of memory that consists in gathering, appropriation and recollection. But deconstruction is precisely *not* the attempt to gather memory and the past: "Above all, it does not think itself as gathering; it never reduces the disjunctive difference ... how can we deny that, for Heidegger, the essence of memory resides primarily, originally in gathering (*Versammlung*)" (MdP: 141). This is why deconstruction is not simply Heideggerian. Heidegger's conception of memory allows for no possibility of irretrievable loss: "Can memory without anteriority, that is to say, without origin, become a Heideggerian theme? I do not believe so. With all the precautions that must be taken here, we cannot erase from the Heideggerian text an indispensable reference to originarity" (MdP: 140).

Like his predecessors, Heidegger also attempts to draw a clear distinction between living memory and its external embodiment in material signs. The art or technology of memorization – writing, monuments and so on – is a mere means for living memory to gather itself. The task of thinking, therefore, is to think living memory without the contaminating influence of such technology. This is the classical division that we have seen at work in the Western tradition, and Heidegger has his own version of it. As Derrida notes: "The Heideggerian argument which operates everywhere to justify this division and hierarchy, when it is reduced to its essential schema, has the following form and can be transposed everywhere: 'The essence of technology is nothing technological'" (MdP: 109). This famous sentence is indicative of the work of the later Heidegger, and highlights his distance from Derrida. By "technology" Heidegger means what Derrida means by writing. Heidegger believes that to think the essence of anything, including, of course, the truth of Being, we have to purify it of all such "technology". And Derrida argues that this single sentence is crucial to understanding Heidegger's work:

> We cannot exaggerate the risk and the gravity of this brief sentence (for example): the essence of technology is foreign to technology. Apparently very trivial, it can yet again put into question, with all of the entailing consequences, the scope of even the most fundamental philosophical gesture. (MdP: 140)

We have seen all this before, of course, in Plato's and Husserl's attempts to separate living memory (*mnesis*) from all memorization (*hypomnesis*): "the art of writing, of 'material' inscription, in short, of all that exteriority which, after Plato we call hypomnesic" (MdP: 107). But as Derrida demonstrates in his reading of the *Phaedrus* and Husserl's *Logical Investigations*, this is an impossible desire. The qualities that make memorization possible

– difference, deferral and death and so on – are the same qualities that make living memory possible. Memorization is never simply exterior to living memory. They are always mutually contaminated by each other as part of the same circular economy.

Heidegger's attempt to draw a distinction between essence and technology repeats this Platonic model. He attempts to purify the thinking of "essence" from the external technology of memorization and writing. But Derrida argues that you can never separate essence and technology. They too are always in a relationship of mutual contamination. The very characteristics that make technology possible are the same characteristics that make the thinking of essence possible. According to Derrida, the essence of technology is *always* technological: "Now in this, at least, deconstruction is no longer 'Heideggerian' ... It is precisely this hierarchy, this limit, this purity, reclaimed by Heidegger, that is *deconstructed*, that deconstructs itself" (MdP: 139).

Derrida's entire philosophy is an attempt to deconstruct this Heideggerian attempt to purify essence of all technology. Derrida argues that we can never purify essence or presence of technology and death. Technology does not stand outside the essence of memory as a mere means for memory to recollect itself. Memory is always inhabited by technology. They cannot be separated. This necessary contamination of memory and technology is what Derrida means by the *archive*.

The archive

We are continually surrounded by archives. Our culture is a culture of memory. From memoirs and songs to official government records, memorials and monuments, we are in a constant process of archiving our past, present and future. In our contemporary age, with email, virtual internet libraries, and all our tele-technologies – telephone, television and so on – our methods of archiving are becoming increasingly sophisticated and ubiquitous. Freud, Husserl and Heidegger are all thinkers of the archive. Heidegger, for example, argues that language is the archive or house of Being. Similarly, Husserl maintains that the original constituting acts of the first geometers and scientists are embedded in the archive of language and tradition. And, of course, for Freud the unconscious is itself an archive of repressed memories and traumas. But Derrida argues that while Freud, Husserl and Heidegger are all thinkers of the archive, they ultimately attempt to separate the essence of the event from the archive that records it: Freud's model of successful mourning attempts to separate and interiorize the ideal form of the love object apart from its incarnate existence; Husserl attempts to separate and intuit the ideal form of meanings from their embodiment in indicative language and the "natural attitude"; and Heidegger attempts to think and purify the essence or truth of Being of all technology.

All three presuppose the logic of Heidegger's claim that the essence of technology is nothing technological. But for Derrida the essence of technology is *always* technological, and the essence of the event is *always* archival. As we shall see, this difference between Derrida on the one hand and Freud, Husserl and Heidegger on the other is not a mere matter of conceptual semantics, a subtle difference that is of little consequence to their overall projects. How we think about the archive and our responsibility to the past has considerable ramifications for Derrida's philosophy, and ultimately determines the work of mourning as an ethics and a politics of memory.

In *Archive Fever: A Freudian Impression*, Derrida defines the etymology of the term archive:

> As in the case of the Latin *archivum* or *archium* (a word that is used in the singular, as was the French *archive*, formerly employed as a masculine singular: *un archive*), the meaning of "archive," its only meaning, comes to it from the Greek *arkheion*: initially a house, a domicile, and address, the residence of the superior magistrate, the archons, those who commanded. The citizens who thus held and signified political power were considered to possess the right to make or represent the law. On account of their publicly recognized authority, it is at their home, in that *place* which is their house (private house, family house, or employee's house), that official documents are filed. The archons are first of all the documents' guardians. They do not only ensure the physical security of what is deposited and of substrate. They are also accorded the hermeneutic right and competence. They have the power to interpret archives.
>
> (AF: 2)

According to Derrida the word "archive" derives from the Greek words for place or home (*arkheion*) *and* the words for law or the right to inspection (*archon*). We have already encountered these terms in Derrida's etymology of the term "economy". Economy too derives from home – "*oikos*" and law or principle of management – "*nemein*". An archive is just another name for economy. In fact, all forms of identity are archives; and like all identities, the archive is postal. An original event is externalized and represented in some form of an archive – a written testimony or monument, for example – the sole purpose of which is to recollect the original event in

97

its purity. The event destines itself to itself via the medium of the archive. This is precisely the theory of language we encountered in Plato and Hegel in Chapter 2. Language in Hegel, for example, is literally a tomb or monument that serves as a means to resurrect living memory. The point is always to separate and recollect the original living memory from the dead monuments of writing.

This too is precisely how Husserl and Heidegger think about language, history and the archive. As we have seen, Heidegger attempts to separate and decontaminate the essence of memory and Being from the technologies of language and memorization. Husserl too strives to separate the original constituting acts of consciousness from their sedimentation in the archives of language and tradition. In his introduction to Husserl's *The Origin of Geometry*, Derrida notes how Husserl acknowledges that the archive of language is a necessary prerequisite for a tradition and the possibility of scientific progress. Husserl provides the example of the discoveries of the early geometers, who, without language as a means to archive their discoveries, would have been unable to communicate their findings to their contemporaries and the scientific tradition. But like Plato, Husserl fears we are reaching a point of "crisis", because we are becoming too reliant on lifeless signs, rather than the original constituting acts themselves. Take the Pythagorean theorem, for example. For Husserl the danger of the archive is that anyone can appeal to the language of the theorem without any knowledge or experience of the original constituting acts that gave birth to it. And so, the task of phenomenology is to reactivate these original acts of consciousness. Like Heidegger, Husserl too calls for the separation of the lived event from the archive, demanding that we privilege the former over the latter.

Again, as we saw in Derrida's readings of Plato and Husserl, writing or the archive is never simply external to speech and living memory. The characteristics that make writing or the archive possible, namely difference, deferral, repetition and death, are the *same* characteristics that make speech possible. This is why Derrida is much closer to Freud when it comes to the archive. Indeed, for Freud our entire psychic economies are archives and traces of repressed traumas and memories, which (contrary to his theories about successful mourning) resist being allotted their proper place and always come back to haunt us. As much as we may try to repress certain memories, to separate them from the archives of memorization, we can never succeed. There will always be traces of memory that resist repression and recollection. So for both Freud and Derrida living memory cannot be separated from the archive that records it. The essence of speech, memory or any lived event is always already archival.

Contrary to Plato and Husserl, therefore, there is no such thing as a pure event that subsequently expresses itself in an external archive. The archive is always already contained within the event and makes it possible: "The archivization produces as much as it records the event" (AF: 17). There is no such thing as an event that is not already an archive:

> [A]rchival technology no longer determines, will never have deter-mined, merely the moment of the conversational recording, but rather the very institution of the archivable event ... Archivable meaning is also and in advance codetermined by the structure that archives. (AF: 18)

This is contrary to how we normally think about archives. We are used to assuming that first an event happens and the archive comes later. But as we have seen, many of Derrida's theoretical points challenge this every-day understanding: archi-writing comes before speech, repetition before identity and so on. Derrida never denies the existence or reality of events. He merely challenges the possibility of thinking an event as somehow prior to the archive that records it. The essence of the event is always archival.

In *Echographies of Television*, Derrida gives numerous examples of how archival technology constitutes the very content that it archives. Television, like all tele-technologies, is a perfect example of a postal economy in that it attempts to destine a living presence over a certain distance (from the Greek *tele* meaning "afar"). A television news network, for example, destines a "live" report across huge distances to a viewing public, which duly receives it in its "immediacy". But according to Derrida, the very possibility of a postal economy is that the letter never arrives. There is never a simple pres-ence, a "live" event that is communicated in its purity. How a news network may film, frame or narrate a "live" report will always determine its content. Two news networks filming the exact same events may communicate two very different broadcasts. This is what Derrida means by *artifactuality*: the idea that actuality is itself an artifact:

> [A]ctuality is, precisely, *made*: in order to know what it's made of, one needs nonetheless to know that it is made. It is not given but actively produced, sifted, invested, performatively interpreted by numerous apparatuses which are factitious or artificial, hierarchiz-ing and selective, always in the service of forces and interests to which "subject" and agents (producers and consumers of actuality – sometimes they are "philosophers" and always interpreters, too) are never sensitive enough. No matter how singular, irreducible, stubborn, distressing or tragic the "reality" to which it refers, "actu-ality" comes to us by way of a fictional fashioning. (ET: 3)

This reminds us of Derrida's phenomenological inheritance. The world or "reality" is never simply given, present and transparent to all. This is not, of course, to deny the existence of reality; it is merely to challenge the conception of reality in terms of presence. For Derrida "reality", or the "event", is always already structured by the archive that records it. Derrida gives the infamous example of the Rodney King videotape, which recorded the severe beating of Mr King by members of the Los Angeles police department. In the trial that followed the beating, both the prosecution and the defence appealed to the same videotape as evidence. The lawyers for the police officers actually attempted to interpret Mr King's actions on the tape as threatening to the police, thereby justifying their own actions. Derrida's point is that even a videotape or a photograph of a "live" event is always an archive, which, by definition, lends itself to interpretation. A picture may tell a thousand words, but it will never reproduce a past event in its lived "immediacy". A picture, like all archives, tells a story. It is an interpretation and will always be selective and incomplete.

Now this has two important repercussions. First, all archives are a form of what Derrida terms "archi-violence". Now, by violence Derrida does not mean violence in the sense of doing physical harm to someone. Violence just means selection and exclusion. Take this book, for example. In selecting certain of Derrida's texts for discussion while excluding others we are engaging in a form of violence to Derrida's work. But this act of exclusion is the very possibility of any kind of selection or decision-making process.

All archives, therefore, are a form of archi-violence: "What is at issue here, ... is the violence of the archive itself, *as archive, as archival violence*" (AF: 7). This means that all archives are evaluative. There is no such thing as a completely neutral or value-less archive. Even the etymology of the word "archive" includes this power of selection and interpretation in the figures of the *archons*. To return to our news network example, the news is never presented in a neutral fashion. All news reporting is a form of archi-violence in that it makes certain decisions, highlighting certain things and excluding others. Even a photograph or a video recording is evaluative in this sense. There is no such thing as a neutral archive for Derrida. All archives are evaluative and, like any form of identity, lend themselves to possible reinterpretation.

This brings us to our second point. If archi-violence is the very possibility of the archive, then the very act of archiving always contains within it the risks of misrepresentation and distortion of the facts. In *Archive Fever* Derrida plays on the double meaning of the French phrase *mal d'archive*, which can be translated both as "archive fever" and the "evil" or "sickness of the archive". By "archive fever", Derrida means the desire for identity, completion and conservation. As a work of mourning, archive fever is the desire to keep the other close, to remember them and do them justice.

The sickness of the archive, however, is that this attempt to conserve or keep memory is always incomplete, and can always be reinterpreted and potentially abused. As we saw in Chapter 2, the very possibility of a written text having a meaning necessarily includes the possibility that the text can be misinterpreted. Of course this does not mean that a text necessarily *will* be misinterpreted, or that we should not take every precaution to make sure that this does not happen. We should always evaluate different interpretations of a text in the singular context of the text itself. But we cannot eradicate the possibility of this risk. Whether we like it or not, it is always possible that someone can distort the meaning of a written text.

A written text is an archive, and the exact same logic applies here. An archive is always a form of violence, and it is always exposed to the risks of misinterpretation and abuse. A news network, for example, can always archive current affairs in such a way as to serve preconceived ideological conceptions. But again, this does not mean that any archive is as good as any other. We can always evaluate different archives contextually. If we were to present a video archive in which we claimed that the Berlin Wall came down in 1986, others would have no difficulty in dismissing this interpretation in the greater context of contemporary Western history, our cultural norms and protocols of dating and so on. Archives never take place in a vacuum. There are always laws and standards by which we can evaluate them. Derrida insists on this refusal to allow an "anything goes" attitude in which even reality itself can be denied:

> Finally, as I suggested too quickly a moment ago, the requisite deconstruction of this artifactuality should not be used as an alibi. It should not give way to an inflation of the simulacrum and neutralize every threat in what might be called the delusion of the delusion, the denial of the event: "Everything," people would then think, "even violence, suffering, war, and death is constructed, fictionalized, constituted by and for the media apparatus. Nothing ever happens. There is nothing but simulacrum and delusion." While taking the deconstruction of artifactuality as far as possible, we must therefore do everything in out power to guard against this critical neoidealism and remember, not only that a consistent deconstruction is a thinking of singularity, and therefore of the event, of what it ultimately preserves of the irreducible, but also that "information" is a contradictory and heterogeneous process. (ET: 5–6)

Unlike many fashionable "postmodernists" who attempt to theorize the real world into non-existence, Derrida never denies the reality of the world and singular events. His point is just that we can only experience these events as archives. Our experience of an event may always be evaluative, it may even be highly erroneous, but that does not mean the event has not happened. But we can only experience events *as* archives. We can never point outside the archive and definitively say "This is *exactly* what happened."

The archive is therefore a work of mourning. It attempts to keep, conserve and recreate the past, while at the same time affirming that it is always incomplete, resisting our efforts to "settle all accounts". And as a work of mourning, archival work is interminable: there can never be a final and definitive archive. To do justice to past events is to continue to archive them by opening them to new possibilities of interpretation. In this way, the past can have a future: "It is a question of the future, the question of the future itself, the question of a response, of a promise and of a responsibility for tomorrow" (AF: 36); "The archivist produces more archive, and that is why the archive is never closed. It opens out of the future" (AF: 68).

To open an archive to the possibility of justice, however, is at the same time to open it to the risks of manipulation and abuse. There can be no possibility of justice without these risks: "this possibility (of abuse) is irreducible, it must remain irreducible, like the very possibility of evil, if responsibility is going to be possible and significant, along with the decision, ethics, justice etc." (ET: 133). We have to affirm the possibility of these risks, not as a means to accept or condone the abuses of memory, but to constantly remind us of our responsibility towards the past.

Similar to Freud, therefore, Derrida's conception of the archive testifies to the impossibility of recollection, the impossibility of separating living memory from the technology that records *and* constitutes it. But again, Derrida discerns a tension between the Freud of catastrophe and Freud the scientist. While the former accounts for the impossibility of repression and recollection and the spectral traces of ghosts and phantoms, the latter does everything in his power to exorcise these ghosts from the domain of scientific reason:

> [A]s classical metaphysician and as a positivist *Aufklärer*, as critical scientist of a past epoch, as a "scholar" who does not want to speak with phantoms, Freud claims not to believe in death and above all in the virtual existence of the spectral space which he nonetheless takes into account. (AF: 94)

In illustrating his point, Derrida recounts the story of Freud's essay "Delusions and Dreams in Jensen's *Gradiva*" (1953–74). *Gradiva* was a novel by Norbert Hanold, an archaeologist who was obsessed by the figure of Gradiva, a woman who was incinerated during the eruption of Vesuvius. On a visit to Pompeii, Hanold discovered a plaster cast of Gradiva's foot which filled him with great pleasure and which he hung in his office. Freud uses the example of Hanold to illustrate his logic of repression as embodied in Hanold's delusional belief that he converses with Gradiva's ghost. Now, while the Freud of death and loss accounts for the ghosts and spectres of memory, the scientific Freud wants to completely exorcise the ghost of Gradiva and "out-archaeologize" Hanold by disclosing in good scientific fashion the "truth" of his condition.

Freud goes on to subject Gradiva's ghost to a successful work of mourning whereby the spectres of both Gradiva and Hanold's obsession are assigned their proper place within a rational scientific description. But Derrida wants to juxtapose the Freud of fracture, death and loss to Freud the *Aufklärer*, who insists on chasing away the ghosts of memory. From Derrida's point of view, the spectres of memory are the very possibility of the future. They testify to the fact that we will never be done with the past: that the task of archival memory is interminably to repeat and reinterpret our past. We can only do justice to the past by opening it up to the possibility of reinterpretation, with all the risks that this necessarily entails.

Take the controversial example of the holocaust. When thinkers like Derrida challenge what we mean by "reality", "events", "historical facts" and so on, it is not uncommon that they are accused of lending weight to historical relativism and holocaust revisionism in particular. Nothing could be further from the truth for Derrida. In claiming that all historical archives – the events of the holocaust, for example – are open to possible reinterpretation is not to deny the singularity of the event itself. Indeed, for Derrida, in order to do justice to the memory of the holocaust we have a responsibility to keep it alive by continually opening it up to new possibilities of interpretation.

The holocaust is an archive like any other historical event. Many historical commentators have called for a prohibition on all interpretations of these terrible events, claiming that the horror of the holocaust is such that it should be beyond all archiving and interpretation. But for Derrida this would be a great injustice to the memory of the dead. We have a responsibility to keep their memory alive by continually retelling and reinterpreting their stories. If we fail to do this, if we fail to take on the responsibility of this archival work, this work of mourning, then their memory may truly be forgotten.

As we have seen, however, the very possibility of this archive fever (*mal d'archive*), this desire to do justice to the dead, is the simultaneous possibility of the evil of the archive (*mal d'archive*). The very act of archiving, of remembrance, runs the risk of itself taking on the form of forgetting and injustice. After a visit to Yad Vashem – Israel's official memorial to the victims of the holocaust – Derrida comments in an interview:

When an archive such as Yad Vashem is established and kept up, an act of piety and of memory is performed to prevent this from being erased. But at the same time, which is ambiguous and horrifying, it is the very act of archivizing, which contributes somehow to classification, relativization and forgetting. Archivization preserves, but it also begins to forget. And it is possible that one day, and one thinks of this with horror, Yad Vashem will be considered as just another monument. Because it is kept, consigned to the exteriority of archives, because it is here between walls, everything has been recorded, a CD Rom was made, the names are on plaques, and so because it is kept, well, it may be lost, it may be forgotten. There is always this risk, and that is the ambiguity of the concept of archive, that I've been concerned with elsewhere, one always runs the risk of losing what one keeps and of forgetting precisely where memory is objectivized in acts of consignment, in objective places.   (YV: 11)

The *mal d'archive* is not only the risk of forgetting but, more disturbingly, it is the risk of the evils of revisionism and the willingness to do an injustice to the memory of the victims. As Derrida argues, however, we cannot do justice to the past without this risk of injustice. This does not mean in any way, shape or form that Derrida condones these revisionist interpretations, or that his theory of the archive lends any credence to them. On the contrary, the very existence of holocaust revisionism only serves to emphasize our infinite responsibility to defend incessantly and urgently, and do justice to, the memory of the dead.

Derrida's theory of the archive therefore does not lend any weight to historical revisionism.[10] It gives an account of how this type of interpretation is possible, but this possibility is at the same time the possibility of doing *justice* to the past and the dead. One archive or interpretation is not as good as any other. False, malicious or ideological interpretations can always be deconstructed and dismissed within a particular historical context.

The worst thing we could do is try to censor or limit all attempts at reinterpreting an event such as the holocaust. It is even self-defeating to attempt to censor the vile pronouncements of holocaust revisionism. To do so not only tends to provide unwarranted publicity to the individuals who espouse such revisionism but, more importantly, any form of censorship also rules out the possibility of doing justice to the victims. So rather than censor revisionism, we should drag it out in the open and, with all the historical resources available to us, expose its historical lies, failures and ideological hatred. To do so is to subject the holocaust to a work of mourning. It is the simultaneous desire to keep the memory of the events and the victims close, while giving their memory the possibility of a future. In this way the voices of the dead will never be silenced. They will continue to haunt us, calling us to responsibility and justice. By attempting to place the holocaust beyond all interpretation and archiving (including the risk of revisionism) we inevitably fall into the trap of the Freudian model of mourning, whereby we "settle all accounts" with the dead. If we were to do so, then the memory of the dead would truly be forgotten and the human race, like Freud, would just simply move on.

Conclusion

In this chapter we have seen how Derrida's challenge to the teleology of memory is foreshadowed in the works of Freud, Husserl and Heidegger. Whereas the figures we encountered in Chapter 2 all think memory in terms of the *telos* of complete and total recollection, Freud, Husserl and Heidegger all think identity and memory in terms of death and repetition. Identity is never simply given. It destines itself to itself in a circular movement of postal recollection. But the circle is always cut. It never comes to completion; and it is repetition, the irreducibility of death and loss, that keeps the circle in motion.

Derrida argues that all three thinkers fail to think repetition in terms of a work of mourning. While Derrida insists that memory is *always* contaminated by death and loss, Freud, Husserl and Heidegger ultimately attempt to separate the "essence" of identity and memory from the technology of writing and the archive.

This difference between Derrida and his predecessors is of considerable importance. It is only because past events and memory are contaminated by writing that we can remember them at all. If we *were* to separate the essence of memory from writing, then we would rule out the possibility of doing justice to the past. It is precisely the impossibility of this separation that makes possible the work of mourning as the desire to give a voice to the dead, and which is why, as we shall see in Chapter 4, the work of mourning is always an ethics and politics of memory.

CHAPTER FOUR

The risks of negotiation: ethics and politics

The work of mourning is always an ethics and a politics of memory. As we have seen, the archive preserves the memory of the past while affirming the fact that memory is always selective and incomplete. There is no such thing as a neutral archive. This means that the question of memory is also a question of responsibility. How we think about identity and the past determines how we think about justice and the future. How we archive the identity of the holocaust, for example, determines our commitment to render justice to the dead. All identity is archival, which means the question of identity is inextricably tied to the ethical and the political.

It has been argued that one can discern a decisive shift or turn towards ethical and political themes in Derrida's later work. Many commentators have attempted to identify an "early Derrida", who concentrated primarily on philosophical and literary texts, and a "later Derrida", for whom the ethical and the political play a central role. But this attempt to identify a theoretical "turn" in Derrida's work fails to take account of the primary role that the ethical and the political have played in Derrida's texts from the very beginning. As we have argued, Derrida's entire body of work can be comprehended as a work of mourning. The work of mourning is essentially the desire to do justice to the *other*. All of Derrida's work can be read and understood in the context of this desire.

By the "other", Derrida just means everything that escapes or resists our attempts at gathering and recollection. The other is not necessarily another person or another thing. The other is the dis-adjustment in adjustment: the absence and loss at the heart of presence and the same. As we have seen, all of our identities attempt to gather themselves by excluding and effacing this relation to the other. But as Derrida consistently demonstrates, our attempts to banish the other to the outside are destined to fail; the other is always already inside us.

Take our own personal identities, for example. All identities are postal in that they destine themselves to themselves *via* their relation to the other: to everything they are not. John Smith affirms his self-identity only by virtue of distinguishing himself from Mary Smith, Robert Smith, Michael Jones and so on. But this relation to the other is never simply external to identity. It is this relation that makes identity possible in the first place: "The other is in me before me" (TS: 84). But while the relation to the other is what makes identity possible, it also renders impossible all claims of self-identity to perfection and completion. While our self-identities may be determined in relation to other people, we can never know what is going on in other people's minds, for example. In contrast to Freud and Hegel, Derrida's work of mourning always affirms the fact that the other, whether living or dead, always resists our attempts to settle all accounts.

Our relation to the other also determines our relation to the past and the future. When deconstruction thinks about the past it attempts to give an account of all the others who have been excluded from our traditional forms of identity, while at the same time thinking the future as an openness to all the unknown others who are yet to come. This affirmation of the other, or what Derrida calls "alterity", is the desire that drives and impassions deconstruction:

> Deconstruction always presupposes affirmation ... I mean that deconstruction is, in itself a positive response to an alterity which necessarily calls, summons, or motivates it. Deconstruction is therefore vocation – a response to a call. The other, as the other than self, the other that opposes self-identity, is not something that can be detected and disclosed within a philosophical space with the aid of a philosophical lamp. The other precedes philosophy and necessarily invokes and provokes the subject before any genuine questioning can begin. It is in this rapport with the other that affirmation expresses itself. (DO: 149)

Despite all our claims to have gathered our identities and the past into a harmonious whole, the catastrophe of memory testifies to the fact that the other is already inside us; like the ghosts of Freud's melancholic, the other resists all appropriation and recollection. And just as the ghosts of the dead summon us to preserve and do justice to the memory of the past, the other calls us to affirm that there is always more work to be done.

All of the figures of mourning that we have encountered: the pharmakon, *différance*, iterability and so on, are singular attempts to take account of this relation to the other, which again is not necessarily another person. In "Signature Event Context", for example, the point of iterability is to open up texts to the other as the possibility of being interpreted otherwise. And these strategic interventions are far from abstract intellectual exercises. As Derrida writes in *Limited Inc.*, "a context is never a gesture that is neutral, innocent, transparent, disinterested" (LI: 131). To intervene in any given context is always to commit to a certain criteria of selection and exclusion. There is no such thing as a neutral intervention: the relation to the other is always an ethical and a political relation.

The task of deconstruction is to attune itself to the call of the other at the heart of identity. This is what Derrida means by *invention*. Derrida plays on the etymology of the word invention (*in-venire*) both in the sense of "making something new" and as "in-coming of the other". To affirm the relation to the other is to give identity new life by opening it up to everything it is not: everything it has excluded (and has been excluded from) in the past, and everything it may be in the future. To invent is to welcome the other, to let the other come. Whether in the figure of a hungry stranger or an unpredictable event, the first gesture of deconstruction is always to say yes to the other:

> The invention of the other is not opposed to that of the same, its difference beckons toward another coming about, toward this other invention of which we dream, the invention of the entirely other, the one that allows the coming of a still unanticipatable alterity and for which no horizon of waiting as yet seems ready, in place, available ... To invent would then be to "know" how to say "come" and to answer the "come" of the other. (PI: 55–6)

Derrida's many neologisms are all attempts at such strategic *intervention*. They all attempt to inhabit a particular context or economy, opening it up to the other and producing something new, which is why, for Derrida, invention is always a form of *hospitality*.

Hospitality

Deconstruction is first and foremost an affirmation and a desire to open up one's home (*oikos*/economy) to the call of the other. This is why the concept of *hospitality* is so central to Derrida's ethical theory. In *On Cosmopolitanism and Forgiveness*, Derrida asks the rhetorical question: "'To cultivate an ethic of hospitality' – is such an expression not tautologous?" (OC: 16). For Derrida, ethics *is* hospitality. All ethics is founded on the relation to the other, on the willingness and the desire to welcome the other into one's home (*ethos*).

> Hospitality is culture itself and not simply one ethic among others. Insofar as it has to do with *ethos*, that is, the residence, one's home, the familiar place of dwelling, in as much as it is a manner of being there, the manner in which we relate to ourselves and to others, to others as our own or as foreigners, *ethics is hospitality* ...
>
> (OC: 16–17)

Following Émile Benveniste, Derrida argues that the word "hospitality" derives from the Latin *hospes*, which itself is derived from *hostis*. Hospitality literally means the power or capability (*potis*) to host the other. The host is someone who has the power to welcome the other while remaining master of his home.

Derrida relates hospitality to the gift. We remember from Chapter 1 that Derrida desires to think an unconditional gift-giving that would shatter all economies of exchange and reciprocity. Normally when we give each other gifts we do so in the full knowledge that we shall get something back. In contrast to this *conditional* gift-giving Derrida desires to affirm an *unconditional* gift-giving, which would expect nothing in return: a giving without reason or explanation. The same logic applies to a conditional and unconditional hospitality. Derrida argues that hospitality is normally understood in terms of an economy of exchange. The host remains master of his domain and welcomes the other only on certain conditions: "Welcome to my home ... please remove your shoes and do not touch the furniture." In turn the guest respects and returns in kind these conditional expectations (gratitude for invitation, bottle of wine, etc.). This is a circular economy of exchange that organizes itself around the mastery of the host. And this does not just apply to individual hosts. Similar conditions determine the hospitality of the city and the nation state: "Welcome to our country ... provided you fulfil certain immigration requirements, restrictions ....".

To this conditional hospitality Derrida wants to oppose an unconditional hospitality that, like the gift, desires to welcome the other without expectation, reciprocity or calculation. Only a hospitality that is impassioned by this impossible desire can ever hope to be genuinely hospitable:

> I have to – and that's an unconditional injunction – I have to welcome the Other whoever he or she is unconditionally, without asking for a document, a name, a context, or a passport. That is the very first opening of my relation to the Other: to open my space, my home – my house, my language, my culture, my nation, my state, and myself. I don't have to open it, because it is open, it is open before I make a decision about it: then I have to keep it open or try to keep it open unconditionally.
>
> (PF)

In the same way that we can only think the unconditional gift from within the conditional economy of everyday gift-giving, however, so too unconditional hospitality can only be thought and pursued in terms of the laws of conditional hospitality. While we *desire* unconditional hospitality as a means to render our conditional laws and institutions more hospitable, we can only do so in terms of our conditional laws. Otherwise we run the risk of reducing this desire to an empty moralizing cliché.

> [Hospitality] wouldn't be effectively unconditional, the law, if it didn't *have to become* effective, concrete, determined, if that were not its being as having-to-be. It would risk being abstract, utopian, illusory, and so turning over into its opposite. In order to be what it is, *the* law thus needs the laws, which, however, deny it, or at any rate threaten it, sometimes corrupt or pervert it. And must always be able to do this. (OH: 79)

While we desire it unconditionally, therefore, in concrete reality we do require certain limits and restrictions on hospitality. We cannot just abandon our borders and see what happens. Our duty as hosts is to negotiate between this law of *unconditional* hospitality and the necessary laws of a *conditional* hospitality:

> It is a question of knowing how to transform and improve the law, and of knowing if this improvement is possible within an historical space which takes place *between* the Law of an unconditional hospitality, offered *a priori* to every other, to all new comers, *whoever they may be*, and *the* conditional laws of right to hospitality, without which *The* unconditional Law of hospitality would be in danger of remaining a pious and irresponsible desire, without form and without potency, and even being perverted at any moment. (OC: 22–3)

This risk of corruption or perversion of hospitality brings us to the second meaning of the term *hostis*. Like the undecideability of the term *pharmakon*, which means both remedy and poison, the term *hostis* means both stranger *and* enemy ("hostile"). An unconditional hospitality desires to welcome *every* other without restrictions. This means that it is always possible that the other whom we welcome into our home may attempt to destroy us. But this is a risk we have to affirm:

> For unconditional hospitality to take place you have to accept the risk of the other coming and destroying the place, initiating a

111

revolution, stealing everything, or killing everyone. That is the risk of pure hospitality and pure gift, because a gift might be terrible too.   (H: 71)

We should always desire *a priori* (prior to any experience and calculation) to welcome every other unconditionally. If your doorbell rings in the middle of the night, your first impulse should be to welcome and come to the aid of the other. But this does not mean that you do not calculate. If the other informs you through the letterbox that he is here to kill you and your family then obviously you do not open the door. So there is an important distinction here between the desire for unconditional hospitality – which should be absolute – and the irreducible necessity in singular contexts of negotiating this desire in terms of the laws of conditional hospitality and making responsible decisions.

If we were to translate the desire for unconditional hospitality into a simple rule – "Welcome everyone without restrictions" – and apply it universally in all contexts, then this would be a form of irresponsibility. We must desire to welcome unconditionally, but this does not absolve us of the responsibility to *negotiate* with the laws of conditional hospitality in singular contexts.

This is the key to Derrida's ethical and political theory and we shall see it again and again in this chapter. Hospitality is a negotiation between the desire for the unconditional, and the necessity of the conditional. Negotiation is another term for the work of mourning. We desire to keep our conditional identities and economies while at the same time letting them go: opening them up to the risks of the unconditional. The work of mourning is the desire to negotiate this double-bind. In any given context, to negotiate means to open up the context to the risks and uncertainty of the unconditional, while negotiating these risks in terms of the singular differences and distinctions that determine it as *this* particular context. The two go hand in hand for Derrida. A hospitality that only calculates with the conditional would be predictable and self-serving; a hospitality that only calculated with the unconditional would be empty and useless.

Justice and the undecidable

Hospitality demands, therefore, that in any given context we must respect that it is this particular context, while affirming the fact that its singularity always exceeds our attempts to enclose it in any one interpretation. This respect for the singularity of contexts is what Derrida means by *justice*.

In 1989 Derrida explored the relationship between justice and the law in response to an invitation by the Benjamin N. Cardozo School of Law in New York to present a paper on the topic "Deconstruction and the Possibility of Justice". The very title of the colloquium seemed intent on provoking Derrida to respond to his many critics who claim that deconstruction has nothing whatsoever to do with justice, the ethical and the political. In his response, "Force of Law: The 'Mystical Foundation of Authority'", Derrida argues that not only does deconstruction concern itself with the possibility of justice, but "Justice in itself, if such a thing exists, outside or beyond law, is not deconstructible. No more than deconstruction itself, if such a thing exists. Deconstruction is justice" (FOL: 14–15).

Derrida makes a key distinction between the law (*droit*) and justice. By the law he means the history of right, of legal systems and institutions. We saw in Chapter 3 how the archive is always a form of violence. Again, violence for Derrida does not necessarily mean physical violence (although with the inauguration of certain laws and institutions this may indeed be the case). Like all forms of identity, the law is also founded on violence as selection and exclusion. Our laws never simply drop from the heavens. The "mystical" foundation of authority and the law is that it is always the effect of a relation to the other, and to all the differences and "others" that are excluded at the origin.

Whereas the law attempts to efface this relation to the other and originary violence by appealing to the conditional, the calculable and the possible, however, justice affirms the relation to the other as the unconditional, the incalculable and the impossible. To do justice, then, is to affirm the disadjustment at the heart of the law.

> So, the law as such can be deconstructed and has to be deconstructed. That is the condition of historicity, revolution, morals, ethics, and progress. But justice is not the law. Justice is what gives us the impulse, the drive, or the movement to improve the law, that is, to deconstruct the law. Without a call for justice we would not have any interest in deconstructing the law. That is why I said that the condition of possibility of deconstruction is a call for justice. Justice is not reducible to the law, to a given system of legal structures. That means that justice is always unequal to itself. It is non-coincident with itself. (VR: 17)

The desire for unconditional justice is the desire to shake the law out of its dogmatic slumbers, to demand of the law that it be more just, "[a]nd deconstruction is mad about this kind of justice. Mad about this desire for justice" (FOL: 25). And just as we must negotiate between the conditional and the

113

unconditional laws of hospitality, so too we must negotiate between the law and everything that exceeds and resists it: "there can be no justice without an appeal to juridical determinations and to the force of law; and there can be no becoming, no transformation, history or perfectibility of the law without an appeal to a justice that will nonetheless always exceed it" (R: 150).

We cannot, therefore, conflate justice with the mere application of rules. An application of a rule may be in accordance with the law and may produce beneficial results, but it would not be an example of justice.

> Law (*droit*) is not justice. Law is the element of calculation, and it is just that there be law, but justice is incalculable, it requires us to calculate with the incalculable; and aporetic experiences are the experiences, as improbable as they are necessary, of justice, that is to say of moments in which the decision between just and unjust is never insured by a rule. (FOL: 16)

Take the example of a judge. A judge must respect and implement the laws. But if they were simply to apply the law universally, without ever taking into account the singularity of different contexts, without ever taking into account the possibility of exceptions to the law, then this would not be justice. A judge can only do justice to the law if she is willing to open up the law to the singularity of each context, to take the risks of reinterpreting and reinventing the law:

> In short, for a decision to be just and responsible, it must in its proper moment if there is one, be both regulated and without regulation: it must conserve the law and also destroy it or suspend it enough to have to reinvent it in each case, rejustify it, at least reinvent it in the reaffirmation and the new and free confirmation of its principle. Each case is other, each decision is different and requires an absolutely unique interpretation, which no existing, coded rule can or ought to guarantee absolutely. (FOL: 23)

The key again is negotiation. While we unconditionally desire justice and hospitality, we can only do so in terms of the law and the conditional: "*both* calculation *and* the incalculable *are necessary*" (R: 150). Our desire for justice is the desire to open up the law to the other, but this openness always risks transforming itself into an empty moralizing. This is why the desire for justice must always negotiate with the law and the conditional.

> You cannot simply call for justice without trying to embody justice in the law. So justice is not simply outside the law, it is something

114

which transcends the law, but which, at the same time, requires the law; that is, deconstruction, transformations, revolutions, reformations, improvement, perfectibility – all that is a process. So even if justice is foreign to the process, it nevertheless requires the process, it requires political action, rhetoric, strategies, etc. What is foreign to strategy requires strategy. That is the double-bind which causes the difficulty. (H: 73)

Anyone, however, can open a context to the risks of the unconditional, and anyone can *claim* to negotiate these risks in terms of the singularity of the conditional. In order to be truly just, therefore, negotiation has to assume the risks of a responsible decision.

According to Derrida, a genuine decision is never the simple application of a law or a rule. Only a decision that passes through what he terms the "aporia of the undecideable" can be called a genuine decision. All this means is that a decision can never be absolutely sure of itself; it should always include an element of risk and uncertainty. And this is the aporia or contradiction: a "decision" is only a genuine decision if it contains an element of "undecidability". For example, if in a particular context I am faced with deciding between option A and option B, and I appeal to a rule or preconception that tells me "In this context always choose option A", then this would not be a genuine decision for Derrida. A genuine decision, on the other hand, might take the following form: "I have negotiated and calculated to the best of my ability, and even though I cannot know with certainty that this is the right decision, I will assume the risks of a qualitative distinction and decide on option A."

When our judge is hearing a particular case, for example, she has a responsibility not merely to collect the evidence and then consult a law manual to tell her what to do. She has to open up the singularity of the case to the risks of the unconditional: to the possibility that the defendant may be an exception to the law, as we normally understand it. But of course she cannot simply accept the word of the defendant and their legal counsel. She has a responsibility to negotiate these risks in terms of the evidence that determines the case as *this* particular case. But negotiation cannot go on forever. Eventually she is going to have to make a decision. This means she will have to assume the even greater risks of a qualitative distinction – innocent or guilty – and commit to that decision. The point here is that the judge can never know with *absolute certainty* that she has made the right decision. No matter how overwhelming the evidence, the judge can only claim to do justice to the case in question if she affirms an element of undecidability at the heart of her decision; she has to allow for the possibility that she could be mistaken. If the judge did claim to know that her decision was the right one then, according to Derrida, this would not be a just decision; it would merely be the application of a rule. Of course, a decision can always be revised, but without this element of risk and the undecidable, there can be no possibility of justice.

We must be careful, however, not to confuse undecidability with indecision. The point of passing through the aporia of the undecidable is to suspend all of our preconceived judgements and opinions, exposing ourselves to the risks and uncertainties of each singular context. But this does not result in indecision. On the contrary, undecidability is the *condition* of a responsible decision:

> Far from opposing undecideability to decision, I would argue that there would be no decision, in the strongest sense of the word, in ethics, in politics, no decision, and thus no responsibility, without the experience of some undecideability. If you don't experience some undecideability, then the decision would simply be the application of a programme, the consequence of a premiss or of a matrix. So a decision has to go through some impossibility in order for it to be a decision. If we knew what to do, if I knew in terms of knowledge what I have to do before the decision, then the decision would not be decision. It would simply be the application of a rule, the consequence of a premise, and there would be no problem, there would be no decision. Ethics and politics therefore, start with undecideability. (H: 66)

"A decision is something terrible" (H: 67); our lives would be much easier if we could just consult a manual to tell us what to do, and what decisions to make in every situation. But in order for a decision to be just, it has to pass through the aporia of the undecidable. But we *do* have to decide. We cannot just give ourselves over to the unconditional and the undecidable. While we have to open ourselves up to other, we still have to negotiate, and we still have to make decisions.

> To be direct, simple and brief, let us say this: a decision is always required immediately, "right away." It cannot furnish itself with infinite information and the unlimited knowledge of conditions, rules or hypothetical imperatives that could justify it. And even if it did have all that at its disposal, even if it did give itself the time, all the time and all the necessary facts about the matter, the moment of *decision as such*, always remains a finite moment of urgency and precipitation, since it must not be the consequence or the effect of this theoretical or historical knowledge, of this reflection or this

deliberation, since it always mars the interruption of the juridico- or ethico- or politico-cognitive deliberation that precedes it, that *must* precede it. The instant of decision is madness says Kierkegaard.

(FOL: 26)

The gift of death

Derrida's invocation of Kierkegaard here is not accidental. In *The Gift of Death*, Derrida follows Kierkegaard in identifying in Abraham a lesson in "the concept of duty and absolute responsibility". When Abraham responds to God's demand that he kill Isaac, he embodies the terrible aporia of the undecidable in that he is willing to sacrifice or "deal death" to the law in the name of justice and responsibility:

> The moral of the fable would be morality itself, at the point where morality brings into play the gift of death that is so given. The absolutes of duty and of responsibility presume that one denounce, refute, and transcend, at the same time, all duty, all responsibility, and every human law. ... Absolute duty demands that one behave in an irresponsible manner (by means of treachery and betrayal), while still recognizing, and reaffirming the very thing that one sacrifices, namely, the order of human ethics and responsibility. In a word, ethics must be sacrificed in the name of duty. (GD: 66–7)

Having suspended the authority of the law, Abraham finds himself in the aporia of the undecidable, whereby he has to negotiate between the conditional law (which commands him not to kill) and the unconditional voice of the other (God) who commands him to sacrifice his son. Abraham does not know what the outcome of his decision will be, but in the midst of this terrible undecidability, this moment of madness, he makes a decision, and responds to the call of the other (God): "'Here I am': the first and only possible response to the call by the other, the originary moment of responsibility such as it exposes me to the singular other who appeals to me" (GD: 71).

Of course, neither Derrida nor Kierkegaard intends us to take the parable of Abraham and Isaac literally. Abraham embodies the unconditional *desire* to sacrifice the law in the name of responsibility and justice, to assume the risks and uncertainty of the undecidable and, most importantly, the necessity of committing to a concrete decision. As the embodiment of the desire and willingness to do justice, Abraham "calculates with the incalculable" to the extent that he responds to the call of the unconditional other. But even though Abraham acts in the name of justice, if he were an actual historical figure we would be well within our rights to question whether he had nevertheless made the *right* decision. If a contemporary Abraham were to attempt to sacrifice his son in response to the call of the "other", we would be morally obliged to send the relevant authorities to intervene on Isaac's behalf. It is always possible that in the name of justice we might make the wrong decision.

The point of the parable for Derrida, therefore, is not that we should imitate Abraham's particular decision to sacrifice his son (indeed we have a responsibility to do justice to Isaac as well); rather, Derrida appeals to Abraham to illustrate his willingness to sacrifice the law in the name of justice. Abraham attempts to do justice to the law by opening it up to the risks and uncertainty of the call of the other (God). He then attempts to negotiate these risks in terms of the singular context in which he finds himself, and faced with the aporia of the undecidable (he cannot know whether he is making the right decision), he assumes the even greater risks of a qualitative distinction (he chooses God over Isaac), and commits, in "fear and trembling", to a concrete decision. This is the real lesson of Abraham: anyone can open up a context to the risks of the unconditional, but genuine responsibility is in assuming the risks of qualitative distinctions and concrete decisions.[1]

What about Isaac? Is Isaac not the other too? Do we not also have a responsibility to respect the unconditional singularity of Isaac as wholly other? According to Derrida we do, which is why he says that "every other is wholly other":

> If God is completely other, the figure or the name of the wholly other, then every other (one) is every (bit) other. *Tout autre est tout autre* … . [This] implies that God, as the wholly other, is to be found everywhere there is something of the wholly other. And since each of us, everyone else, each other is infinitely other in its absolute singularity, inaccessible, solitary, transcendent, nonmanifest, originarily nonpresent to my ego … then what can be said about Abraham's relation to God can be said about my relation without relation to every other (one) as every (bit) other, in particular my relation to my neighbor or my loved ones who are as inaccessible to me, as secret and transcendent as Jahweh. Every other (in the sense of each other) is every bit other (absolutely other). (GD: 66)

This is why "a decision is something terrible" (H: 67). In any given context we will be duty bound to respond to every other as wholly other. But of course this is impossible. As Derrida notes in *The Gift of Death*, when I feed my cat every morning I am sacrificing all the other cats that may be starving in the world. We cannot do justice to every other in every context. While we should *desire* unconditionally to always treat every other as wholly other, in determinate contexts we will always have to choose. This is why Kierkegaard's reading of the Abraham parable is so important to understanding Derrida's ethical and political theory.[2] Only a decision that endures the aporia of the undecidable can be called a responsible decision. To return to our previous example, if our doorbell rings in the middle of the night, our first desire should always be to welcome the other, but we still have to negotiate. In certain contexts we have a responsibility to assume the Abrahamic risks of a qualitative distinction and say no to this particular other.

Every other is wholly other

Derrida's invocation of "every other is wholly other" is indebted to the influence of the work of Emmanuel Levinas, a Lithuanian-born French philosopher, who came to prominence as the first person to introduce systematically the work of both Husserl and Heidegger to France. At the heart of his work is the claim that "ethics is first philosophy". For Levinas, the relation to the other (ethics) precedes and makes possible the relation to identity and the self. In his magnum opus, *Totality and Infinity* (1969), Levinas argues that we have a responsibility to affirm and do justice to the "infinite" transcendence of the other, which always resists the attempts of the philosophical tradition to assimilate everything to the "totality" of presence (ontology) and the same.

While Levinas undoubtedly had a considerable influence on Derrida's work, there are vital and significant differences between them. If observed from the point of view of each author's critique of Hegelianism, these differences become apparent. This is evident in Derrida's confrontation with Levinas in "Violence and Metaphysics",[3] where Derrida attempts to challenge Levinas's reading of Husserl and Hegel. Ostensibly, Levinas's objection to Hegel is similar in tone to that developed by Derrida. Levinas is critical of the Hegelian attempt to view the relation to the other as a mere means to recollect the self: the self passes through the other (not-self) in order to recollect itself in its original presence; the singularity of the other is nothing more than a moment in the dialectic of the same. Levinas considers Hegel to be promoting the "concreteness of egoism", or a desire that is motivated by a will to make the other "my" alter ego. The way to escape such narcissistic egoism, according to Levinas, is through an affirmation of the other as "absolutely other": as "the Stranger who disturbs the being at home with oneself [*le chez soi*]" (Levinas 1969: 39).

The other as absolutely Other emerges in and through the ethical relationship I have with the other in what Levinas terms the "face-to-face" encounter. In the face-to-face encounter, the self does not determine the nature of the other in terms of commonality or analogy (the other as *my* other) but in terms of its *absolute* dissimilarity, its irreducible and infinite transcendence. This signals the truly ethical moment between the self and the other that Hegel never takes account of:

> Ethical subjectivity dispenses with the idealizing subjectivity of ontology which reduces everything to itself. The ethical "I" is subjectivity precisely in so far as it kneels before the other, sacrificing its own liberty to the more primordial call of the other. For me, the freedom of the subject is not the highest or primary value. The heteronomy of our response to the human other, or to God as the absolutely Other, precedes the autonomy of our subjective freedom. As soon as I acknowledge that it is "I" who am responsible, I accept that my freedom is anteceded by an obligation to the other.
>
> (DO: 63)

Such a notion of responsibility, which takes the form of a response to the other who "precedes the autonomy of our subjective freedom", would not be alien to Derrida's own ethical theory. Much of what Levinas writes on the primordial call issued by the other has inspired and influenced not only Derrida but a host of contemporary thinkers. Derrida's objection, therefore, is not aimed at the main thrust of Levinas's work.

Derrida does see a problem, however, in Levinas's contention that the other is somehow *totally* asymmetrical, *totally* different, or absolutely exterior. In a discussion of Husserl's "Fifth Cartesian Meditation" and its relationship to Levinas's thought, Derrida launches a critique of this Levinasian thesis. His argument centres around Levinas's claim that Husserl's notion of "analogical appresentation", whereby we comprehend the ego of the other as analogous to our own, ends up reducing the other to the same; that is, Levinas contends that when Husserl argues in favour of analogical appresentation as the way the other as other becomes present to my ego, he ignores the other's undelimitable transcendence. For, as Derrida remarks, "to make the other an alter ego, Levinas says frequently, is to neutralize its absolute alterity" (WD: 123).

In this context, Derrida's defence of Husserl *contra* Levinas is significant in that it strikes a blow, albeit subtle, at the heart of the Levinasian project, one that, it might be argued, Levinas struggled all his life to recover from.

Derrida neatly synthesizes the core of his disagreement in the following paragraph:

> [Husserl] is concerned with describing how the other as other, in its irreducible alterity, is presented to me ... For it is impossible to encounter the alter ego (in the very form of the encounter described by Levinas), impossible to respect it in experience and in language, if this other, in its alterity, does not appear for an ego (in general). One could neither speak, nor have any sense of the totally other, if there was not a phenomenon of the totally other, or evidence of the totally other as such. No one more than Husserl has been sensitive to the singular and irreducible style of this evidence, and to the original non-phenomenalization indicated within it.   (WD: 123)

As we saw in Chapter 3, Husserl does not argue that the other is reducible to the same. In the very act of appearing, the other *qua* alter ego shows itself to be somewhat "non-phenomenalizable": my experience of it will always be partial and incomplete. But to be recognized as other at all, requires that the other be somewhat *known* to the ego, for if the other were not similar (analogical) to the ego, the ego would have no way of identifying it as other. The upshot of Derrida's argument is that what is absolutely other is only absolutely other because we experience it as such. "To make the other an alter ego", therefore, far from "neutralizing its absolute alterity", allows its alterity to be affirmed.

It is only as a result of recognizing sameness that we can say yes to the other. In "Violence and Metaphysics", Derrida writes of the other as "the stranger" (following Levinas in this), whose singularity is irreducible to full objective scrutiny, but who must be recognized *as* stranger for this to be ascertained:

> The stranger is infinitely other because by his essence no enrichment of his profile can give me the subjective face of his experience from his perspective, such as he lived it. Never will his experience be given to me originally, like everything, which is *mir eigenes*, which is *proper* to me. This transcendence of the nonproper no longer is that of the entirety, always inaccessible on the basis of always partial attempts: transcendence of *Infinity*, not of *Totality*.   (WD: 124)

According to Derrida, Husserl legitimizes his use of the term "totally other" by virtue of the fact that he acknowledges "an intentional modification of the ego" through analogical appresentation. Levinas, on the other hand, refuses to entertain such a modification. To do such a thing "would be a violent and totalitarian act for him". Consequently, Levinas "deprives himself of the very foundation and possibility of his own language"; that is, "What authorizes him to say 'infinitely other' if the infinitely other does not appear as such in the zone he calls the same?" (WD: 125). This question calls Levinas to account for his belief that the otherness of the other is in some sense infinite, that it is already outside or exterior to the order of the same.

The alter ego, argues Derrida, is somewhat the same, in that it is an ego, and yet it is other by virtue of the fact that it too can say "ego" or "I". The other (alter), in saying "ego", separates itself from all other egos in the same space:

> The egoity of the other permits him to say "ego" as I do; and this is why he is Other and not a stone, or a being without speech *in my real economy*. This is why, if you will, he is a face, can speak to me, understand me, and eventually command me. Dissymmetry itself would be impossible without this symmetry, which is not of the world, and which, having no real aspect, imposes no limit upon alterity and dissymmetry – makes them possible, on the contrary. This dissymmetry is an *economy* in a new sense; a sense which would probably be intolerable to Levinas.   (WD: 125–6)

Derrida expresses here what he has not ceased to enunciate in many different ways and forms since his early confrontation with Levinas, and most especially in his treatment of the gift: we are always already caught inside a tradition or a circular economy; we are claimed by forces, such as language and the law, that precede us and determine our beliefs and practices. There can be no escape from the circle or economy of exchange; we can push against its limits, but we are incapable of going outside it into some absolutely exterior site. In Derrida's language, we can strive after the gift, but once the gift is presented it is simultaneously annulled. Derrida could very well be asking Levinas in this context, as he asks his reader in *Given Time*, to "give economy a chance". For it is only in being with the other that we can recognize the other as other, as one whose singularity is irreducible to my phenomenological gaze. The relation to the other is always negotiated in terms of the same.

The question of Hegel also marks a point of divergence between Derrida and Levinas. While Derrida agrees with Levinas's rejection of the teleological impetus of Hegel's logic, when it comes to the issue of how we relate to the other Derrida recognizes a certain indispensability in Hegel:

> The other, for me, is an ego which I know to be in relation to me as an other. Where have these two movements been better described

than in *The Phenomenology of Mind*? The movement of transcendence toward the other, as evoked by Levinas, would have no meaning if it did not bear within it, as one of its essential meanings, that
in my ipseity [power to say "I can"] I know myself to be other to
the other.   (WD: 126)

We are always embedded in determined conditional contexts. Hegel's
genius lay in showing how identity is formed in and through mutual recognition between conscious beings in such contexts. Individuals, that is, come
to a knowledge of themselves only by recognizing themselves as the other
of other individuals (Hegel called this the master–slave dialectic). Hegel and
Husserl, therefore, while always in need of deconstruction for their respective tendencies towards absolute knowledge and pure eidetics, are two fundamental sources of the specifically Derridean approach to the question of
the other. We can see how clearly Derrida appreciates this in one of his most
anti-Levinasian statements concerning the nature of "narcissism":

There is not narcissism and non-narcissism; there are narcissisms
that are more or less comprehensive, generous, open, extended.
What is called non-narcissism is in general but the economy of a
much more welcoming, hospitable narcissism, one that is much
more open to the experience of the other as other. I believe that
without a movement of narcissistic reappropriation, the relation to
the other would be absolutely destroyed, it would be destroyed in
advance. The relation to the other – even if it remains asymmetrical,
open, without possible appropriation – must trace a movement of
reappropriation in the image of oneself for love to be possible, for
example.   (P: 199)

For Derrida, therefore, the "wholly other" is not *absolutely* other" in
Levinas's sense. It is the otherness that becomes apparent in and through
the dialectic of ego and alter ego. The individual, that is, comes to know
that the other is irreducibly incommensurable with the order of the same,
or comes to the realization that there is something secret or non-manifest
about the other, not because the other is "*infinitely* other", but because the
alter ego's experience of the world is different from the ego's, for the simple reason that they say "I" from two different perspectives. When Derrida
speaks of the need for narcissism he is merely reiterating this point. Unless I
can identify myself to a certain degree in the other, how can I come to love
that other? There can indeed be non-narcissism in moments of self-abandon
and sacrifice. Such is what occurs in the case of Abraham. But this does not
mean that Abraham escapes the economy of exchange and reappropriation

totally; in saying yes to the other he welcomes the foreign in a moment of madness. Abraham does, however, remain within the economy. He is both inside and outside the law (economic and legal): he is never exterior to it in any absolute sense.

This again is what Derrida means by negotiation. We can only account for the relation to the other as wholly other, in terms of narcissism and the same. Like Abraham, we always have to negotiate the desire for the unconditional (the pure gift, pure hospitality, pure identity, pure presence, etc.) from within the limits of a conditional economy. In attempting to abandon the conditional altogether, Levinas essentially repeats the Heideggerian logic that "the essence of technology is nothing technological". Having reified the other to an absolute and infinite degree, Levinas deprives himself of the ability to negotiate with any determinate, concrete, actual others. Contrary to his best intentions, for Levinas the essence of ethics is nothing ethical.

Derrida, however, is adamant that ethics (the relation to the other) is always ethical: it always negotiates with determinate conditional others. As Hegel argues in his *Phenomenology*, the relation to the other is always determined in terms of the same, and vice versa. Indeed, for Hegel the master–slave dialectic is a *struggle* for recognition, even to the death. While Levinas wants to purify the other of all struggle and conditionality, for Derrida, following Hegel, the relation to the other is never immune from struggle or what he calls *polemos*. "*Polemos*" is the Greek word for "warlike", from which we derive the word "polemic". Derrida maintains that the relation to the other is always inscribed in *polemos*, in struggle, conflict and violence:

> There is *polemos* when a field is determined as a field of battle because there is no metalanguage, no locus of truth outside the field, no absolute and ahistorical overhang; and this absence of overhang – in other words, the radical historicity of the field – makes the field necessarily subject to multiplicity and heterogeneity. As a result, those who are inscribed in this field are necessarily inscribed in *polemos*, even if they have no special taste for war.
>
> (TS: 12)

The fact that all meaning – all identity, ethics and politics – presupposes a relation to the other, means that we are always inscribed in *polemos*. While Derrida unconditionally desires that we respect "every other as wholly other", he argues:

> As far as this formula is concerned, I think that everyone agrees, no one can seriously protest against it or rebut it, but it makes no

difference – *difference*, the differend, and consequently a war and polemics are not only possible, they are *the necessary result* of this agreement that *tout autre est tout autre*.   (TS: 58)

Derrida therefore follows Hegel in arguing that the relation to the other is never neutral; it can never be purified of violence and struggle, which means at certain times we are going to have to make difficult choices. While Levinas relates to every other on his knees, head lowered in a sense of religious awe, Derrida recognizes that the relation to the other always has to be negotiated in terms of *polemos* and the same; that while we unconditionally *desire* that every other is wholly other, there will be times, in certain contexts, when we may have a responsibility to kill the other.

There is no such Abrahamic moment in Levinas. From a Levinasian perspective, the axe-murderer is as "wholly other" as his victim. Having purified his analysis of all *polemos*, risk and undecideability, Levinas's conception of the "Other", or "Infinite", precedes all ethical and political totalities: the essence of his ethics is nothing ethical. So while there are many parallels between Derrida and Levinas, particularly in their shared desire that "every other is wholly other", there is ultimately a divergence of thought that is so profound that it must be stressed and taken account of in any attempt to situate these two thinkers within a common context and conversation.[4]

The politics of identity

It is important at this point to distinguish Derrida's understanding of the relation to the other from the many claims and strategies of what has come to be called the postmodernist "politics of identity". By the "politics of identity" we mean the proliferation in recent decades of philosophical theories that all claim to espouse the rights of minority groups: feminism, race theory, queer theory and so on. Now, while Derrida argues that we should always fight to correct injustices, particularly where minorities are concerned, the proponents of the politics of identity very often presuppose a logic that is diametrically opposed to Derrida's notion of responsibility.

We remember once again that, for Derrida, to do justice to any context is to desire to open it up to the unconditional. This means that we suspend all of our preconceived notions and prejudices, and from within the context itself strive to push against its conditional limits, opening it up to the risks and promise of a future. But this is the easy part. Derrida insists that we then have to negotiate and qualify these risks in terms of the singularity of the context itself, which means – like Abraham – assuming the risks of qualitative distinctions and concrete decisions. To absolve ourselves of this responsibility is to yield to an abstract conception of the law whereby everything is calculated and programmed in advance.

Derrida himself was well aware of how his own appeals to the unconditional could be abused in this way: "Taken in themselves, alone, without any other contextualization, without supplementary discourse and precautions, they can become politically quite dangerous and compromised with that which should have been avoided: 'opening to the other' has already become a moralizing and unpalatable stereotype ..." (N: 194). It is not enough to desire simply that "every other is wholly other". This desire must always be negotiated in terms of the context under discussion. This is the only way we can fulfil our responsibility to distinguish different others in different situations, and our failure to do so can have ethical and political consequences that are nothing short of disastrous. This is why Derrida distances himself from many of the claims and strategies of the politics of identity. While Derrida insists on negotiating the desire for the unconditional in terms of the singularity of the event, the proponents of the politics of identity often do the opposite.

Rather than assume the risks of qualitative distinctions, they *level* all distinctions and differences in the name of abstract concepts such as "tolerance" or "rights". Derrida has nothing against the desire for tolerance and rights *per se*, but if we translate this desire into a simple rule – "Be tolerant to everyone in every circumstance" – and apply that rule universally, then this would be a form of injustice. In concrete situations we have to assume the risk of making distinctions between different "others", the axe-murderer and his potential victim for example. To appeal simply to abstract notions, applying them universally in all contexts is to risk nothing. Anyone can appeal to an abstract universal notion of "rights" or "tolerance". It requires a lot more of people to address themselves to the singularity of a context, exposing themselves to the aporia of the undecidable and committing to a decision.

The proponents of the politics of identity, however, often *absolve* themselves of all risk and undecidability, and merely replace one law – only be tolerant to such and such a group – with another – be tolerant to everyone regardless of the context.[5] But according to Derrida this translates the desire for the unconditional into "an act of good conscience and irresponsibility – and thus it is indecision, profound inactivity beneath the appearance of activism or resolution" (P: 361). So while Derrida is very sympathetic to all of these individual causes in principle, he is highly critical of any attempt to absolve ourselves of the duty to negotiate. No matter how "revolutionary" or "liberating" the rhetoric, to efface the singularity of a context in the name of an abstract law is, for Derrida, the ultimate form of injustice. There can be no responsibility or justice without the risks of negotiation.[6]

Mourning, spectres and the democracy to come

Derrida's ethical theory, his conceptions of hospitality and justice, risk, responsibility and commitment, is at the heart of his politics. As we noted earlier, negotiation is a work of mourning in that it attempts to keep the singularity of the conditional while opening it up to the risks of the unconditional. As a work of mourning, Derrida's political theory desires to preserve the political values and institutions of the past while opening them up to the risks and promise of the future. In addition to the themes we have already addressed, Derrida's political theory also emphasizes the issues of inheritance, the "messianic" and the "democracy to come". When it comes to politics, Derrida demands that we not only have a responsibility to welcome the other who greets us at our door, we also have a responsibility to render justice to all those spectral others who are no longer, and are yet to come.

In *Specters of Marx: The State of the Debt, the Work of Mourning, and the New International*, Derrida informs his reader that he intends to speak about ghosts:

> I am getting ready to speak at length about ghosts, inheritance, and generations of ghosts, which is to say about certain others who are not present, nor presently living, either to us, or outside us, it is in the name of justice ... No justice seems ... possible or thinkable without the principle of some responsibility, beyond all living present, with that which disjoins the living present, before the ghosts of those who are not yet born or who are already dead ... (SM: xix)

Derrida, that is, wishes once more to address the question of justice as something that is not yet, whose time is not of the present, for such a time is only that of "laws and rights". The time of justice is the time of those who have long since passed (*revenants*) and those whose time is still to come (*arrivants*). Derrida pledges himself to a "politics of memory, of inheritance, and of generation".

In contrast to a traditional political ontology, which thinks its concepts, its history, its laws and institutions in terms of presence and recollection, Derrida writes: "[w]e are attempting something else ... we are directing out attention to the effects or the petitions of a survival or of a return of the dead" (SM: 187 n.7). Rather than assuming the identity of our political and ethical institutions as simply given, Derrida proposes a *hauntology*, which affirms the fact that the spectral other is always inside us, that our institutions are always haunted and disturbed from within. Whereas Freud attempts to exorcise his analysis of all ghostly remains, Derrida's hauntology

127

insists that we must: "learn how to talk with [ghosts] how to let them speak or how to give them back speech, even if it is in oneself, in the other, in the other in oneself; they are always there, specters, even if they do not exist, even if they are no longer, even if they are not yet" (SM: 176). We must desire to give an unconditional hospitality not only to the living, but also to the dead. We have a responsibility to open our homes, our laws and our identities to the call of these spectral "others". The very possibility of hospitality and justice depends on our ability to speak with ghosts.

Specters of Marx opens with a reflection on Shakespeare's *Hamlet*, Act 1, Scene 5. In this scene the ghost of Hamlet's father returns to inform his son of the injustice that led to his untimely death: "I am thy father's spirit, Doomed for a certain term to walk the night/And for the day confined to fast in fires/Till the foul crimes done in my days of nature/Are burnt and purged away." The ghost imparts to Hamlet an injunction and a responsibility to do justice, and departs crying "Adieu, adieu! Hamlet, remember me."

Like Abraham, who responds to the unconditional call of the other ("Here I am"), Hamlet also responds to the injunction of the other to render justice:

Hamlet: ... Swear.
Ghost [*beneath*]: Swear. [*They swear*]

God's demand of Abraham that he kill Isaac knocks Abraham's world off course. The call of the other shatters all his preconceptions and expectations, confounding his understanding of justice and the law. But in a moment of madness Abraham assumes the risk and uncertainty of God's impossible demand and commits to a concrete decision. The call of the other also confounds Hamlet's understanding. His world is knocked off its hinges and, responding to the call of his father's ghost, he too commits (however reluctantly) to a decision: "The time is out of joint: O cursed spite, That ever I was born to set it right!"

Derrida is particularly fond of this Shakespearean insight. He too argues that the "time is out of joint": living presence is always inhabited by traces of difference and deferral; dis-adjustment is always at the heart of adjustment; time and memory are always partial and incomplete. But, like Hamlet, Derrida still desires to recollect and do justice to the past; he still desires to "set it right". But without this temporal fracture, without this openness to the other that exceeds and resists all our attempts to adjust it, there could be no possibility of justice:

It seems to me ... that at the heart of justice, of the *experience of the just*, an infinite disjunction demands its right, and the respect of an irreducible dissociation: no justice without interruption, without divorce, without a dislocated relation to the infinite alterity of the other, without a harsh experience of what remains forever *out of joint*.   (FWT: 81)[7]

Derrida maintains that we always experience the call of the other and the injunction to render justice, in the form of an inheritance. As Hamlet inherits and affirms the demand for justice from the ghost of his father, so too we have a responsibility to inherit and affirm the demands for justice that have been bestowed on us by the many ghosts who haunt our political past. But again, this desire to respond to the other, to the unconditional demand for justice, has to be negotiated. An inheritance, like an archive, is always selective: "An heir is not only someone who receives, he or she is someone who chooses, and who takes the risk of deciding" (FWT: 8). We must inherit the demands of the past, but that does not absolve us of the responsibility of submitting our own particular inheritance to rigorous critique and of distinguishing one inheritance from another:

An inheritance is never gathered together, it is never one with itself. Its presumed unity, if there is one, can consist only in the injunction to reaffirm itself by choosing. "One must" means one must filter, sift, criticize, one must sort out several different possibilities that inhabit the same injunction.   (SM: 16)

Our responsibility to do justice to the other cannot absolve itself of the duty to select and filter, to assume the risks of contextual distinctions and concrete decisions. The desire for justice, the desire to inherit and do justice to the past, has to negotiate itself in terms of the singularity of the inheritance that is handed down to us: "Inheritance is never a given, it is always a task" (SM: 54). Derrida summarized his position during a roundtable discussion in Dublin:

In the case of Hamlet, I try to show in *Specters of Marx* that the responsibility in front of the father's call, for it to be a responsibility, demands that choices be made; that is, you cannot remember everything for a fact; you have to filter the heritage and to scrutinize or make a close reading of the call. This means that to inherit, or to keep memory for a finite being implies some selection, some choice, some decision. So the son has to make a decision; even if he wants to be true to the father, or to remember the father, as a finite being he has to select within the heritage and that is again the question of undecideability.   (H: 67)

129

An inheritance is never simply given. The task of historical memory is not reducible to simply allocating the events of the past their proper place. The time of the past, like the time of the present, is always "out of joint", and we inherit this temporal disjunction in the form of an injunction: as the demand to render justice to the past and to "set it right". This structural dis-adjustment, this openness towards the other and the future, is what Derrida means by the "messianic".

Derrida contrasts his use of the term "messianic" with its traditional use as an article of religious faith. By the messianic Derrida does not mean the coming of a particular "Messiah" who will deliver the "chosen people" of a determinate faith. Derrida conceives of the messianic as a universal structure, an opening towards the promise and uncertainty of the future, that affirms our responsibility to inherit and do justice to the past: "This universal structure of the promise, of the expectation of the future, for the coming, and the fact that this explanation of the coming has to do with justice – that is what I call the messianic structure" (VR: 23). The messianic is the dis-adjustment at the heart of all identity and memory that makes it possible for the other "to come". And this coming of the other can take the form of a new interpretation, an unforeseeable event, or an actual other calling for asylum at our borders.

Derrida expresses this messianic hope for a more open and more hos-pitable future as the desire for a "democracy to come". The "democracy to come" affirms the injunction that we never be done with democracy. Regardless of how open and inclusive our democratic institutions become, they too are out of joint and open to the risks and demands of the future. But Derrida insists that the "democracy to come" is not simply the interminable aspiration towards a deferred ideal, or the simple acknowledgement that we can always do better (cf. R: 73). These sentiments can easily be trans-lated into excuses for doing nothing. Like the ghost of Hamlet's father, who haunts and disturbs his every waking moment, the "democracy to come" should *threaten* and disturb our sense of complacency and self-assurance:

> The expression "democracy to come" does indeed translate or call for a militant and interminable political critique. A weapon aimed at the enemies of democracy, it protests against all naïveté and every political abuse, every rhetoric that would present as a present or existing democracy, as a de facto democracy, what remains inad-equate to the democratic demand, whether nearby or far away, at home or somewhere else in the world, anywhere that a discourse on human rights and on democracy remains little more than an obscene alibi so long as it tolerates the terrible plight of so many millions of human beings suffering from malnutrition, disease and

humiliation, grossly deprived not only of bread and water but of equality or freedom, dispossessed of the rights of all, of everyone, of anyone.   (R: 86)

The "democracy to come" is therefore not merely a dream or an ideal. To affirm it is to affirm the disjunction at the heart of all our democratic institutions as the injunction that demands justice in the urgency of the here and now. Derrida responds to this injunction in calling for the inauguration of a "New International", a "global solidarity" that demands a "profound transformation, projected over a long term, of international law, of its concepts, and its field of intervention" (SM: 84). The New International is the political articulation of Derrida's ethic of hospitality. As a work of mourning, Derrida's ethical and political theory expresses this desire to do justice to the memory of the past, and to the living and the dead.

Negotiation and risk

In this final section we shall endeavour to evaluate Derrida's overall contributions to contemporary ethical and political theory. While we firmly believe that Derrida has an immense amount to contribute to contemporary debates, we would also argue that his position has relative strengths and weaknesses. In order to elucidate these points we shall attempt to situate Derrida in terms of the ongoing exchange between the American pragmatist Richard Rorty and the German critical theorist Jürgen Habermas, specifically in regard to their respective reflections on the role of the political in Derrida's work.

In his "Habermas, Derrida, and the Functions of Philosophy" (1998b), Rorty writes: "I think of Jacques Derrida as the most intriguing and ingenious of contemporary philosophers, and of Jürgen Habermas as the most socially useful – the one who does the most for social democratic politics" (1998b: 307). While the disciples of both Derrida and Habermas have traditionally viewed each other as adversaries – a productive personal and professional relationship only blossomed between them in the last years of Derrida's life – Rorty sees their work as essentially complementing each other.[8]

According to Rorty, the key to understanding the differences between Derrida and Habermas is in recognizing the fact that they belong to different spheres of philosophical endeavour. On Rorty's reading, Habermas is a "public" philosopher while Derrida is a "private" one. By "public" Rorty means someone who is concretely engaged in the problems and issues that arise in day-to-day democratic politics. A public philosopher is someone who is less interested in big theories about identity and language, and more interested in forming practical initiatives to improve health services or the welfare state. It is precisely Habermas's investment in such practical and everyday political concerns that, for Rorty at least, defines the value of his work for contemporary political philosophy.

Derrida, on the other hand, is an exemplary example of what Rorty terms a "private ironist". Rorty contrasts what he means by the ironist approach to philosophy to that of the "metaphysical". By the latter, Rorty means the various attempts of philosophers over the centuries to gain access to the "true reality" of things behind appearance and contingency. The metaphysician is someone who is driven by the conviction that there is an overriding Truth to human existence. The task of the philosopher is to gain access to this fundamental truth and to put it into action. The idea is that once we get a grasp on the "big picture", once we get the overarching theory right, then all of our problems will be solved in due course.

The ironist is someone who challenges the very presuppositions of this position. As Rorty himself writes, "Roughly, the ironist is a nominalist and historicist who strives to retain a sense that the vocabulary of moral deliberation she uses is a product of history and chance – of her being born at a certain time and a certain place" (1998b: 307). Rorty's ironist is someone who agrees with Derrida's claim that all identity is contextual; that all our attempts to recollect our identities are subject to the vicissitudes of temporality and history. We can never recollect the "big picture" or the "true reality" of things. But it is precisely this impossibility that drives and inspires us to use our imaginations to construct and create a better and more comprehensive understanding of who we are and the world around us. So whereas, for Rorty, the public philosopher immerses himself or herself in the practical affairs of everyday political life, the private philosopher is someone who proposes "idiosyncratic projects of self-overcoming" (ibid.). The ironist is someone who suggests new and original ways of looking at ourselves, providing us with inspirational examples of personal and private self-transformation.

According to Rorty, therefore, reading Derrida will not help us in addressing the concrete problems of public democratic life, but it will help each of us as individuals to completely re-evaluate how we think about the world; Derrida may well change your life, but he will not help you decide how to vote. But Rorty believes that we desperately need the Jacques Derridas of this world. We need the original and controversial ideas and visions of private thinkers such as Derrida to challenge and provoke our customary ways of thinking about things. Habermas, on the other hand, has a very different reading of Derrida.

According to Habermas, Derrida belongs in the tradition of what he terms the "philosophy of the subject", a tradition that he believes to have begun with Kant and Hegel and that stresses the "egoism" of the individual subject over questions of social responsibility. But whereas the German Idealist tradition attempts to maintain at least a semblance of a relationship between individual autonomy and social justice, with Nietzsche an awareness and concern for social responsibility is dispensed with altogether. Ever since Nietzsche, Habermas argues, the proponents of the "philosophy of the subject" are obsessed with their own autonomy and individuality; the question of autonomy supersedes all questions of solidarity and social emancipation.

Habermas wishes to counter this tradition with a "philosophy of intersubjectivity". As Rorty writes, "This sort of philosophy will keep what is still usable in Enlightenment rationalism while jettisoning both metaphysical attempts to 'ground' this rationalism in the 'nature of the subject' and ironist attempts to 'subvert' it" (1998b: 309). Central to Habermas's project is the attempt to rescue the true character of dialectical reason from the instrumental rationalism of the Enlightenment. Following Theodor Adorno and Max Horkheimer, Habermas argues that the task of dialectical reason is to overcome man's sense of alienation by projecting utopian possibilities of social emancipation and the reconciliation of man and nature.

Contrary to the "philosophy of subjectivity", which locates rationality in an individual consciousness, Habermas locates rationality in intersubjective discourse; a discourse that aims at the universal validity of unrestricted communication. By "unrestricted communication" Habermas means what he calls an ideal speech situation: a democratic system of communication in which everyone will be allowed the opportunity to take part in a public discourse aimed at a rational and mutual understanding. The task of philosophy then is to remove all obstacles, all distortions and restrictions, that stand in the way of achieving this sense of universal consensus.

The "philosophy of intersubjectivity" has no interest in "presence" or "Being", or any of the other allegedly "private" concerns of philosophers such as Derrida and Heidegger. If the task of critical theory is to remove the obstacles that obstruct the possibility of a shared public discourse, then Habermas argues that what Derrida calls the critique of logocentrism is a turning *inwards* towards the subject rather than a turning outwards to the public and the demands of democratic life. As far as Habermas is concerned, Derrida's primary concerns – presence, identity, memory and so on – have nothing whatsoever to do with a practical and rational political philosophy. Rorty cites the following quotation from Habermas to summarize the latter's summation of the "philosophy of subjectivity":

> A more viable solution suggests itself if we drop the somewhat sentimental presupposition of metaphysical homelessness, and if we

understand the hectic to and fro between transcendental and empirical modes of dealing with issues, between radical self-reflection and
an incomprehensible element prior to all production – that is to say,
when we understand the puzzle of all these doublings for what it
is: a symptom of exhaustion. The paradigm of the philosophy of
consciousness is exhausted. If this is so, the symptoms of exhaustion should dissolve with the transition to the paradigm of mutual
understanding.
(Habermas 1987: 296; quoted in Rorty 1998b: 310)

Rorty cannot follow Habermas's claim that Derrida represents a philosophy of "exhaustion". Where Habermas sees exhaustion, Rorty sees vitality.
According to Rorty, Derrida is a thinker who continually opens up our conventional modes of thinking to unforeseen possibilities and the future. It is
thinkers like Derrida who keep us on our toes and open to the challenges
– and occasional threats – of progress and innovation. Rorty views the difference between Derrida and Habermas as the difference between a Jewish
and a Greek approach to philosophy. Whereas Habermas is primarily driven
by Greek values, such as universality and reason, Derrida is impassioned
by the Jewish values of justice and hope. Rorty captures his point nicely in
the following quote:

I am tempted to follow Derrida in thinking of such hope as marking
a fundamental difference between the Jews and the Greeks. I take
Platonism and Greek thought generally to say, The set of candidates
for truth is already here, and all the reasons which might be given
for and against their truth are also already here; all that remains is
to argue the matter out. I think of romantic (or, for Derrida, Judaic)
hope as saying, Some day all of these truth candidates, and all of
these notions of what counts as a good reason for believing them,
may be obsolete; for a much better world view is to come – one in
which we shall have wonderful new truth candidates. If one holds
the Greek view, then it is reasonable to define truth in terms of idealized rational acceptability in the manner of Habermas, Pierce, and
Putnam. But that definition will be useless once one starts thinking
of languages and truth-candidates as constantly in the process of
change.   (Rorty 1996: 50–51)

Rorty believes that the strength of Derrida's "private" philosophy is that
it helps us to overturn outdated worldviews, including the worldview that
gave rise to the "philosophy of subjectivity", which Habermas accuses
Derrida of promoting. Whereas Habermas reads Derrida as a bad *public*

philosopher, Rorty reads him as a good *private* philosopher, an important distinction that Habermas fails to comprehend.

Rorty insists on this separation of the public from the private. Failure to do so, he argues, is usually what gets philosophers into trouble. The public philosopher who concerns herself with day-to-day democratic politics, for example, should not allow herself to be distracted by such questions as the meaning of Being, of Truth, or Identity. Such questions tend only to muddy the waters and sidetrack the public philosopher from the task at hand. Similarly, the private philosopher should not attempt to translate his theories into public policy. The private philosopher should serve as an example of the liberating power and imagination of self-creation and transformation, but he should not attempt to impose this private conception of self-creation on others.

According to Rorty, however, the greatest threat that emerges from confusing the public and the private comes from the private metaphysicians (as distinct from the private ironists such as Derrida). The private metaphysicians are all those who, thinking themselves to have bypassed all contingency and history, claim to have discovered the "true essence" of human nature and civil society. For these people, the inspirational models of self-creation provided for us by the private ironist are not enough. As Rorty comments, these people "want a world in which all things have been made new and in which the rearrangement of little private things, the pursuit of idiosyncratic autonomy, is subsumed under some higher, larger, more thrilling communal goal" (1998b: 324). Thinking themselves to have discovered the true nature of things, these thinkers then attempt to sweep away everyone and everything that stands in the way of making their vision a reality; a desire that manifested itself in the twentieth century in the form of fascism and Stalinism. As history has taught us time and again, there is nothing more politically dangerous than a philosopher with a "big idea".

The irony of all this is that it is not Derrida but Habermas – the exemplary model of the public philosopher – who runs the risks of falling in league with the private metaphysicians. If the defining characteristic of the latter is their claim to have escaped contingency and history, then Rorty views Habermas's calls for "universal validity" and a communicative rationality that would transcend all conditionality as just more (albeit less threatening) examples of the metaphysical "big idea". On Rorty's reading, we need to complement Habermas's more metaphysical leanings with a sober dose of Derridean irony. Habermas's public philosophy would be far better served, Rorty contends, if he took a page from Derrida's book and, leaving all claims to universal validity behind him, kept his public philosophy separate from the private altogether.

As we noted above, Derrida himself was well aware of how such notions as "every other is wholly other" when translated into a "big idea" can have disastrous consequences in the public sphere. This is precisely why Rorty believes that Derrida too should just stick to what he is good at in the private sphere without attempting to translate it into the public. We should appreciate Derrida for what he can inspire in us as private individuals, but when it comes to the day-to-day practices and procedures of democratic life, we should simply look elsewhere.

We believe there is considerable value in Rorty's analysis. We agree that Derrida was not a public philosopher in the sense that Rorty wishes to attribute to Habermas. While we think that Derrida has some very useful contributions to make to political theory, the simple truth is that if you need a thinker to help you address specific political problems, then Derrida will be of little use to you. However, we would contest Rorty's claim that Derrida is *solely* a private philosopher for three reasons. First, Derrida was actively involved in a wide variety of causes and political debates throughout his career, and his involvement was not simply extra-curricular. He actively campaigned for the release of Nelson Mandela and aligned himself with the Czech dissident intellectuals of the Jan Huss Association in Prague, which earned him a night in jail.[9] He wrote and spoke openly about numerous political problems ranging from Algeria to the Israel–Palestine question, from the rights of asylum seekers to the death penalty and animal rights.[10] He was also a founding member of the research group for the teaching of philosophy GREPH (Groupe de recherche sur l'enseignement philosophique), and campaigned tirelessly for university reform and the teaching of philosophy in the French education system.[11] In these instances Derrida *was* able to use his theories to suggest concrete and practical political initiatives.

Secondly, we believe, following Derrida, that, although useful to a point, there are limits to Rorty's public–private distinction. It will come as no surprise to the reader that, given Derrida's talent for complicating allegedly clear-cut distinctions, he would challenge Rorty on this point. In conversation with Rorty in Paris in 1993, Derrida remarks that the very texts that Rorty takes to be Derrida's most "private" expressions – *Glas* and *The Post Card*, for example – were in fact intended by Derrida to *complicate* the public–private distinction:

> There are a number of examples: in its way the question of the family in Hegel discussed in *Glas*, of the relation of the family to civil society and the state, can be seen as a performative elaboration of the private on a theoretical, philosophical and political plane; it is not a retreat to private life, *La Carte Postale*, the very structure of the text, is one where the distinction between the public and the private is rightly undecideable. And this undecideability poses

philosophical problems to philosophy, and political problems, such as what is meant by the public and the political itself ..."

(RDP: 79)

Of course, Derrida would also argue that the public realm, no less so than the private, is also dependent on the powers of memory. The catastrophe of memory, the impossibility of total recollection and transparency, structures both the private and the public, and renders problematic the attempt to neatly separate them.

Thirdly, we would argue that while Derrida was not a public philosopher *per se*, we believe that his theory of negotiation is an innovative and welcome contribution to public political discourse. Of course, the point of negotiation is not to provide us with concrete responses to determinate problems *à la* Habermas, but rather, to demand of us that we assume the risks and responsibility of determining these responses for ourselves. If a politician were to ask you "How can I improve on our health services?", the response "Well, you must address the singularity of the context, take the risks of qualitative distinctions and commit to a concrete decision" will not be the answer they are hoping for. But this response demands the necessary conditions for anything resembling a responsible decision. And given the tendency in so much of our contemporary public discourse to absolve ourselves of this responsibility, we genuinely believe that Derrida's theory of negotiation is a significant contribution that goes far beyond the "private" concerns of self-transformation.

However, we believe there were also times when Derrida failed to put his own theory of negotiation into practice: when his private inclinations arguably got the better of him. Recall that in order to do justice to any context, whether philosophical, cultural, political and so on, Derrida argues that we have to address ourselves to the *singularity* of the context.[12] A responsible interpretation will always attempt to negotiate between the *unconditional* singularity of the context – the fact that it always resists our attempts to "settle all accounts" – and its *conditional* singularity – the fact that it is *this* particular context. As Derrida himself reminds us:

> For me the place of the political is the place of *negotiation* between, let's say, the open set of present or presentable data such that I can attempt to analyze them (always a finite analysis), and this "democracy to come," which always remains inaccessible, not only as a regulating ideal but also because it is structured like a promise and like a relation to alterity, because it never possesses the identifiable form of the presence or of the presence to self. But the event of that promise takes place *here*, *now*, in the singularity of a here-now ...
>
> (N: 179–80)

137

It is not enough, however, simply to open a context to the unconditional or the "other". The strength of Derrida's analysis lies in his insistence that we negotiate this demand in terms of the singularity of the context, which means always taking account of qualitative distinctions and committing to concrete decisions.

When Derrida reads a philosophical text, for example, he desires to open it up to the unconditional, to the risks and possibility of new and exciting readings. But this desire for the unconditional has to negotiate with the conditional limits of the text in question, taking account of the singular differences and distinctions that determine the text as this particular text. We cannot absolve ourselves of this responsibility by appealing to some abstract law of "infinite interpretability". No matter how much we may desire it or how fashionable it might be, we cannot read whatever we like into a Platonic dialogue, for example. But while Derrida masterfully applies the theory of negotiation to philosophical texts, we believe that when it comes to political contexts there are times when Derrida fails to make important contextual distinctions, with the result that the power of his innovations become entangled in a moral ambiguity, which, we believe, is contrary to the spirit of his work.

In defence of this claim we point to the following three examples to illustrate Derrida's inconsistency in putting his theory into practice: (i) Derrida's insistence on the necessity of Marx, specifically as an antidote to the "evils" of liberal capitalism and the "hegemony" of the United States; (ii) certain of Derrida's reactions to the terrorist attacks on the United States of 11 September 2001; and (iii) Derrida's decision to align himself with Noam Chomsky in his *Rogues: Two Essays on Reason*.

To take our first example, in *Specters of Marx* Derrida attempts to conjure the ghost of a certain Marxism, which, he believes, is synonymous with the desire for justice and the "democracy to come". At times, however, Derrida goes so far as to argue that the name of Marx is a *necessary* prerequisite for the desire for social justice, that "this gesture of fidelity to a certain spirit of Marxism is a responsibility incumbent, to be sure, on anyone" (SM: 90). Derrida writes:

> It will always be a fault not to read and reread Marx … It will be more and more a fault, a failing of theoretical, philosophical and political responsibility … Not without Marx, no future without Marx, without the memory and the inheritance of Marx: in any case, of a certain Marx, of his genius, of at least one of his spirits.
> (SM: 13)

It is one thing to conjure a certain spirit of Marx as a manifestation of the desire for social justice, but it is quite another to argue that the name of

Marx is necessary to articulate this desire. There are many other names, and many other spectres, who also conjure the desire for social justice but without the ideological and political baggage that destined Marxism to historical and political disaster.

Like many European intellectuals, however, Derrida seems to assume the necessity of this Marxist inheritance. While other political theorists and activists have managed to express and embody an unconditional desire for social justice without any appeal to Marx, for countless intellectuals the invocation of Marx is nothing short of a necessary rite of passage. We believe this assumption leads to certain oversimplifications and stereotypes in Derrida's reading. In *Specters of Marx*, for example, Derrida conjures a certain spirit of Marx to counter the triumphalism of what he calls the "new world order". Derrida defines this "new world order" in terms of the "dominant discourse" (SM: 51) of a triumphalist liberal-capitalism, which, in the wake of the fall of communism, claims to have exorcised the ghost of Marx for once and for all. Derrida argues that in a euphoria of self-congratulation, this "dominant discourse" not only attempts to enforce its "global hegemony", but also strives to "disavow", and "hide from", all the injustice and inequalities that continue to exist in the world (SM: 52).

It is not the case that to disavow the name of Marx is to disavow the desire for social justice and the responsibility to address inequalities. If Derrida wants to ascribe this sense of disavowal to individual figures or works (he signals out Francis Fukuyama's *The End of History and the Last Man* (1992)) then we can evaluate each of these claims in their respective contexts. But even individual cases do not warrant the claim that "[n]o one, it seems to me, can *contest* the fact that a dogmatics is attempting to install its worldwide hegemony in paradoxical and suspect conditions" (SM: 51). Derrida goes on to argue that the new world order is not only determined in terms of the hegemonic "dominant discourse" of triumphalist liberal-capitalism, but specifically in terms of "the hegemony of this new world, I mean the United States, [which] would still exercise a more or less critical hegemony, more and less assured than ever" (SM: 40). While this rhetoric of "hegemony" and "dominant discourses" is typical of the conspiratorial theorizing of a certain spirit of Marxism (particularly when it comes to the United States), it lacks the sensitivity and respect for distinctions that characterizes Derrida's other ethical and political writing.

Derrida goes on to list what he terms the "ten plagues" of this "new world order". These plagues comprise a list of social, political and economic problems, ranging from unemployment and homelessness, economic wars, the spread of nuclear weapons and foreign debt. Derrida does not lay the blame for these "plagues" solely at the feet of the United States and liberal capitalism but, given the fact that he characterizes this "new world order" in terms of the global hegemony of the United States, he overlooks any and all contextual details and distinctions that would complicate such a claim, and in a text that calls for the necessity of re-reading Marx, his analysis certainly does not offer any suggestions or insights that could be characterized as specifically Marxist.

Of course, we are not suggesting that liberal capitalism and the United States are immune from criticism when it comes to the social and political problems we are faced with every day. If Derrida desires to open up these singular contexts – foreign debt, unemployment and so on – to the unconditional then he has every right to do so. But he still has a responsibility to negotiate this desire in terms of the singularity of the contexts themselves. But Derrida does not do this. There is no attempt here to qualify any of these claims in terms of a detailed analysis of their respective contexts.[13]

Our second example is Derrida's response to the events of the terrorist attacks on the United States of 11 September 2001. In a lengthy interview with Giovanna Borradori, which was conducted in New York less than six weeks after the strikes, Derrida unreservedly condemned the attacks and recognized the urgency of aligning himself with those who are opposed to "this unleashing of violence without name" (PT:113). However, in the course of the interview Derrida appeals to a number of responses to these events, which, lacking qualification, result in precisely the type of moral ambiguity that his ethical and political theory is supposed to oppose. These responses include the claims that to fight terrorism is to "work to regenerate" it (PT: 100); that the West "recruited, trained and even armed" the terrorists (PT: 115); that one man's "terrorist" is another man's "freedom-fighter" (PT: 104); and that all states (not just the Taliban, for example) "harbour" terrorist organizations (PT: 101). All of these claims demand contextual qualification. Failure to do so, as Derrida himself insists, inevitably results in the abstract levelling logic of moral equivalence. For example, to state that "one man's terrorist is another man's freedom-fighter" without any attempt at qualitative distinction is not even an example of moral equivalence; it is to align oneself with those whose interests are served precisely by the blurring of these distinctions (whether it is the interests of an anti-Americanism that attempts to shift the blame for the terrorist attacks from al-Qaeda leader Osama bin Laden to the United States, or the interests of bin Laden himself).

The standard reaction to this argument is to object "But I'm not drawing a moral equivalence – I'm merely stating the facts", and in the course of the interview Derrida himself appeals to this logic:

> A "philosopher" would be one who seeks a new criteriology to distinguish between "comprehending" and "justifying." For one can

describe, comprehend, and explain a certain chain of events or series of associations that lead to "war" or to "terrorism" without justifying them in the least, while in fact condemning them and attempting to invent other associations. One can condemn unconditionally certain acts of terrorism (whether of the state or not) without having to ignore the situation that might have brought about or even legitimated them. (PT: 106–7)

As Derrida argues elsewhere, however, there is no such thing as a neutral description or "comprehension" of the "facts". As we saw in Chapter 3, facts are archives, and archives are the result of selection and interpretation and always demand contextual qualification. As his own theory clearly states, if someone has an interest in doing justice to the events of 11 September 2001, if someone wants to open its archive to the unconditional – to the risks of interpretation including alleged explanations and so on – then they have a responsibility to qualify these claims in terms of the singularity of the event itself. To appeal to an abstract law of neutral description or "comprehension" is to absolve oneself of this responsibility.

When Abraham is faced with the decision to respond to the call of the other he does not merely assess the facts. In the singular context in which he finds himself, Abraham endures the risks of undecidability and commits to a decision. But such Abrahamic moments are lacking here. Derrida is right that to simply state the claim "One man's terrorist is another man's freedom-fighter" is not to justify it. But by failing to qualify such a claim in terms of the singular context of 11 September 2001, Derrida fails to meet the demands of his own ethical and political theory.

Our third and final example is Derrida's decision to endorse certain of Chomsky's views in his *Rogues: Two Essays on Reason*, a reflection on the notions of sovereignty and the nation state, which was inspired by the United States' use of the term "rogue states", and which appeared in French in 2003, on the eve of the Iraq War (Second Gulf War).

While Derrida is a thinker of the singularity of the event, of the necessity of affirming the risks and uncertainty of the undecidable, Chomsky is a thinker of the law. According to Chomsky, all political events can be reduced to the fact that there are two competing forces in the world: on the one hand, a hegemonic corporate American imperialism, and on the other, *anything else* that claims to "resist" it. In the same way that his linguistic theory attempts to explain language acquisition in terms of abstract, logical structures, so too Chomsky's political theory attempts to explain everything in terms of the abstract law of this either–or logic. There is no singularity of the event in Chomsky; everything is determined in advance. If Chomsky were to live for another hundred years and write another hundred books, we could easily predict exactly what each of these books would say. We would just have to program the relevant proper names, dates, locations and so on into Chomsky's formula and await the results. Indeed, Chomsky is an exemplary example of someone who perpetually absolves himself of the responsibility to address the singularity of contexts, appealing instead to the "neutral" description of "facts" and the abstract levelling logic of moral equivalence. There is no risk, no responsibility, and no possibility of Derridean justice in Chomsky's analysis.

Furthermore, we saw in our discussion of the archive how all identity is founded on an archi-violence. Identity gathers itself to itself by violently excluding everything it is not. In the final pages of the chapter "(No) More Rogues", Derrida argues that all "sovereignty" is similarly founded on violence and the "abuse of power":

> As soon as there is sovereignty, there is abuse of power and a rogue state. Abuse is the law of use; it is the law itself, the "logic" of a sovereignty that can reign only by not sharing. More precisely, since it never succeeds in doing this except in a critical, precarious and unstable fashion, sovereignty can only tend, for a limited time, to reign without sharing. It can only tend toward imperial hegemony. To make use of the time is already an abuse – and this is true as well for the rogue that I therefore am. There are thus only rogue states. (R: 102)

Now, all this is consistent with Derrida's understanding of identity. But once again Derrida fails to make any qualitative distinctions between all these "rogue" states. There are only rogue archives, but that does not mean we do not have a responsibility to distinguish one from another. The archive of the holocaust survivor is not morally equivalent to the archive of the revisionist, and we have an obligation to make clear that distinction. So while all states may have "rogue" origins, there is no risk and no responsibility in failing to make a qualitative distinction between the United States on the one hand and Saddam Hussein's Iraq on the other. But Derrida argues instead for the "intrinsic necessity of rendering useless the meaning and range of the word *rogue*" (R: 103). This is the unfortunate and disappointing conclusion of Derrida's analysis.

Earlier in *Rogues* we have a better example of negotiation at work. One of the key concepts in *Rogues* is "auto-immunity". By "auto-immunity" Derrida means the dis-adjustment or incompletion at the heart of all identity. All forms of identity are auto-immune in that they never completely close in on themselves. They are literally immune to the possibility of their own completion and recollection.

Just as the catastrophe of memory drives and makes possible our desire to do justice to the past, so too auto-immunity is the very possibility of opening up identity to the other and the possibility of justice. But this opening towards the other is *simultaneously* the possibility of injustice. The auto-immunity of the archive, for example, testifies to the possibility and risks of doing both justice and injustice to the past. The two go hand in hand for Derrida: there can be no possibility of justice without the simultaneous threat of injustice. Auto-immunity therefore is "the threat or the danger, the default or the failure, the running aground or grounding, but also the salvation, the rescue and the safeguard, health and security" (R: 123). Like the *pharmakon*, auto-immunity accounts for the possibility of both poison and remedy, good and evil:

> In this regard, autoimmunity is not an absolute ill or evil. It enables an exposure to the other, to what and to who comes – which means that it must remain incalculable. Without autoimmunity, with absolute immunity, nothing would ever happen or arrive; we would no longer wait, await, or expect, no longer expect one another, or expect any event. (R: 152)

Auto-immunity is therefore both the possibility of opening identity to the promise of a future and the possibility of exposing identity to what Derrida terms an "auto-immune suicide". Take democracy, for example. The "democracy to come" embodies the desire for justice not only as an openness towards the other, but also because it contains within itself the endless possibility of its transformation and reinterpretation. It is:

> ... the only system that welcomes in itself, in its very concept, that expression of autoimmunity called the right to self critique and perfectibility. Democracy is the only system, the only constitutional paradigm, in which, in principle, one has or assumes the right to criticize everything publicly, including the idea of democracy, its concept, its history, and its name. (R: 86–7)

But if we attempt to immunize ourselves from this relation to the other (literally to immunize ourselves from our own auto-immunity) then the very possibility of democracy itself is put in jeopardy. When a democracy attempts to close off this openness to the other (which is the very condition of democracy) then democracy commits suicide: "that strange behavior where a living being, in quasi-*suicidal* fashion, 'itself' works to destroy its own protection, to immunize itself *against* its 'own' immunity" (PT: 94).

In developing this idea of an "auto-immune suicide", Derrida cites as "typical of all the assaults on democracy in the name of democracy" (R: 33) the example of Algeria in 1992 when, fearing the election of a radical Islamist party, the state and the leading party suspended the electoral process. What is particularly interesting about Derrida's analysis here is that he does not simply echo the cries of "Hypocrisy!" that predictably erupted from within the ranks of European intellectuals at the time. As Derrida argues, in order to do justice to this particular event we have to be willing to open it up to the risks of the unconditional – including the possibility of threatening the "normal" democratic process – while at the same time negotiating these risks in terms of the singularity of the event itself. What we should *not* do is forego these risks by appealing to some abstract law or conception of "democracy". There is no risk, no responsibility, and no possibility of justice in appealing to abstract pre-programmed notions of "democracy" or anything else. And, as Derrida argues, surely the emergence to power of a group or party whose express intent is to "abolish the normal functioning of democracy or the very democratization assumed to be in progress" (R: 31), is itself another form of auto-immune suicide? How could we claim to do justice to democracy, indeed to commit ourselves to a "democracy to come" if we do nothing to protect democracy from producing the means of its own destruction?

Derrida's point is that while the suspension of the electoral process could indeed turn out to be a possible threat to democracy, it cannot be simply *assumed* that this risk is itself an injustice. The very possibility of doing justice to democracy presupposes the possibility of this threat. So whether or not the suspensions of the election were in fact unjust remains to be argued. All of the differences and distinctions that determined the singularity of this particular context would have to be taken into account before anything resembling a responsible decision could be made.

Democracy like any other form of identity is incomplete "interminable in its incompletion" (R: 38) and open to reinterpretation. What is perceived as a threat to democracy may in fact render justice to democracy.[14] When Derrida reads a philosophical text, for example, it would be unjust and irresponsible to assume that just by virtue of the fact that he attempts to open the text to the risks and uncertainty of new interpretations (which is always to "threaten" traditional readings), that it necessarily follows that his reading is unjust. One can only evaluate Derrida's reading in the context of the text itself. Similarly, one cannot simply assume that a perceived threat to democracy is necessarily an injustice. Of course it does not follow that it is necessarily just either, but this is precisely what remains to be negotiated.

This sort of reading is Derrida at his best, a good example of how his theoretical writings can have provocative and practical effects in the public sphere. So how then are we to account for his inconsistency in applying his own theory? We believe that when it came to determinate political contexts there were times when Derrida's private inclinations – a romantic nostalgia for Marx, for example – conflicted with the demands and rigour of his *own* theory. While we do not believe that these instances take away from the power of Derrida's theory of negotiation, we do think that they serve as a constant reminder to pay heed to Rorty's warning about the consequences that often follow from attempting to mix the public with the private.

Conclusion

In the final assessment, Derrida comprehends the question of the ethical and the political – as he comprehends all his work – in terms of the work of mourning: he desires both to keep and preserve the past, while opening it up to the risks and promise of the future. It is important to stress that Derrida *is* a philosopher of the future. His notion of the "democracy to come" is a constant demand for improvement and openness to what is "to come". This should not, however, be understood simply as an ideal goal; a distant sense of perfection to which we all can aspire. The point of emphasizing the future, for Derrida, is that it should always disturb and threaten us in the present (R: 82). The "democracy to come", the desire to affirm the risks of responsibility and improvement, is never more urgent and necessary than when we are inclined to resist it.

The "democracy to come", however, is not a "big idea" in Rorty's sense of the term. Derrida does not claim to have discovered the truth of human nature or political society, and he does not believe that all of our past values and institutions need to be swept aside in preparation for their realization. When it comes to the political, Derrida is not a radical philosopher. Unlike many of his contemporaries, who look to the spirit of the Bolsheviks or the Jacobins for their political inspiration, Derrida belongs firmly within the reformist political tradition. Like Socrates, Derrida desires to constantly antagonize the *polis* – making plenty of enemies along the way – but he always does so out of a deep respect for the city and its laws. His desire is always to reform and improve our institutions, not to destroy and replace them.

The most important intellectual figure in Derrida's work is ultimately Hegel. As we have seen throughout this book, Derrida was constantly pitting himself against the enormity of his Hegelian inheritance. It is to Hegel that Derrida owes the importance of the themes of history and memory, and of gathering and preservation. As we have seen, for Hegel all identity is historical, and the driving momentum of his philosophical system is the attempt to gather everything into an organizing whole, to preserve everything in an act of all-embracing memory. Now while Derrida is severely critical of all pretensions to gather everything into an all-embracing totality – whether in its Hegelian or Heideggerian guise – he never renounces the desire for gathering and preservation altogether. As a work of mourning, we remember, Derrida desires both to *keep* and *let go*. Derrida is only ever interesting in criticizing what he wants to keep and preserve.

When it comes to the ethical and the political, however, the exemplary figure for Derrida will always be Abraham. Abraham embodies the defining features of Derrida's theory of negotiation – singularity and risk, qualitative distinction and commitment – always emphasizing the necessity of negotiating the risks of the future in terms of the past; that openness to the "other" must always be negotiated in terms of economy and the "same". In our discussion of the gift in Chapter 1, we noted how we are always inscribed in determinate economies – linguistic, cultural, political, religious and so on – but that these economies are always cut; they are always marked by the traces of everything that resists and remains outside them. This sense of belonging and non-belonging is embodied for Derrida in the figure of the Jew. Like the mark of circumcision, the Jew testifies to the sense of belonging to a determinate custom, law and faith, while at the same time testifying to a nomadic sense of non-belonging, of being cut away from the security of the home (*oikos*).

For Levinas, the Jew is interminably lost, forever wandering the desert without any determinate sense of home or the law. Lacking all sense of belonging, without any strong connections to the home and the past, Levinas's ethical sentiments fail to register on the radar of actual human experience. For Derrida, however, Abraham does not represent the wandering Jew. Abraham *is* cut away from his homeland, he does embody the figure of what Derrida terms the "*émigré*", but Abraham always negotiates this sense of detachment in terms of custom, the family and the home. One of the key moments in the book of Genesis is when Abraham purchases the field of Machpelah from the Hittites in the land of Canaan to use as a burial plot for his departed wife Sarah (Genesis 23). The significance of this event highlights not only the fact that while Abraham represents the figure of the *émigré* he also recognizes the importance of the home and tradition (he purchases the burial plot not only for himself and Sarah, but for all his descendants), but that this site of belonging and non-belonging, of keeping and letting go, is also a site of mourning and death.

Like Abraham, Derrida is also detached from the self-assurance of the *oikos* and prepared to affirm the risks of everything that the future may have in store. But again like Abraham, Derrida insists on always negotiating this sense of detachment, this openness to the other, in terms of the concrete bonds of custom and the home. As the work of mourning consistently reminds us, we can only be critical of what we love the most. This, we believe, is the enduring legacy of Derrida's ethical and political theory.

Afterword

Jacques Derrida died on 8 October 2004. What, in the end, is his legacy to the history of ideas? There are those, many eminent philosophers among them, who believe that Derrida was a charlatan undeserving of his fame and importance. One such person is English philosopher Roger Scruton. In his book *Modern Culture* (2005), Scruton argues that Derrida's deconstruction has become:

> ... the pillar of the new establishment, and the badge of conformity that the literary apparatchik must now wear. But in this it is no different from other subversive doctrines: Marxism, for example, Leninism and Maoism. Just as pop is rapidly becoming the official culture of the post-modern State, so is the culture of repudiation becoming the official culture of the post-modern university.
>
> (Scruton 2005: 138)

We are not unsympathetic to Scruton's analysis, for we believe Derrida's postmodern literary disciples have done untold damage to standards right across the academy. What makes their influence so pernicious is that they have misused Derrida's work in an attempt to strike at Western culture. The postmodern elite thinks that deconstruction amounts to an inversion of traditional hierarchies for its own sake. Thus, in their schema, everything white, Western, male and religious is bad. That has led to a belief among students that the great Western literary canon ought to be repudiated, because those who sought to oppress the wretched of the earth produced it. The result is that only literature derived from minorities is now deserving of serious study.[1]

That wanton destruction of value, convention, and tradition, however, is not what Derrida aimed at. The reason his postmodern heirs make those claims is because most of them have little real grasp of Derrida's true aims.

149

They believe that his critique of the book, for example, means laying waste to the Western literary tradition in favour of fragments by outsiders and underdogs. In that, however, they are seriously mistaken. Yes, it is true that Derrida endeavoured to deconstruct the book. But texts such as *Glas* or *The Post Card*, were simply devices to highlight how philosophers are ineluctably situated in an historical matrix from which they cannot escape. They are, in other words, unable to transcend time and place in order to assume a God's-eye standpoint on the essential nature of reality. All philosophers are victims of the catastrophe of memory. Their books cannot give us an accurate picture of our origins because that would mean fully recollecting the past – something Derrida rightly perceives as being impossible.

As we have shown, however, the impossible is Derrida's guiding ideal. Just because we cannot shake off our limits does not mean we should not try to push against those limits. That is why, for him, people like Hegel, Heidegger and Freud are pivotal. Their attempts to reach absolute knowledge, retrieve Being in its primordial splendour and overcome the work of mourning are spectacular examples of a passion for the impossible. Of course, it is left up to Derrida to demonstrate how those attempts failed, and why they will always inevitably fail. But that does not mean that he did not consider them to be exemplary instances of philosophical profundity.

Therein lies the difference between Derrida and most of his disciples. Derrida never sought an end to the book. That, for a man who wrote so many of them, would have been a foolhardy objective. Rather, he aimed to reveal how his favourite authors failed to appreciate the consequences for philosophy of the faultiness of memory and the incompleteness of identity. If, as he maintained, all communal, political and personal identity is encoded in texts, traces, archives and writing, our quest for certainty and self-presence is unachievable. But demonstrating why Hegel's books fail in their ultimate objectives does not mean that Derrida did not admire either the author or his works. Derrida wrote lovingly about most major figures in the Western canon, from Plato to Shakespeare to Joyce. He would never have subscribed to the view that those pillars of the tradition should be ground into dust. If anything, his work is an invitation to read them ever more closely and respectfully than we have hitherto. That is what Derrida did, even while exposing their wilder assertions to rigorous scrutiny.

In short, it is simply wrong to say that Derrida is a postmodern radical who sought the destruction of everything we hold dear in the West. Moreover, unless you view Derrida as someone rooted squarely within the Western tradition, he will make little sense. That is why we have urged that he be read first as a thinker of identity. If one approaches him as such, he will appear less strange and controversial. You will then see him as a kind of latter-day Hegel, in so far as he believes that philosophy is never done in a vacuum but in particular contexts.

But whereas Hegel understands history as the product of ahistorical forces pushing us towards a pre-destined goal or *telos*, Derrida dismisses that as philosophical hype. He does not believe that we can recollect ourselves from the multilayered historical matrices in which we are always already rooted. He thereby follows Kierkegaard in stressing time and chance over historical certainty and permanence. Both Derrida and Kierkegaard are situated, thus, both inside and outside Hegel's system. They embrace his historicism while rejecting his teleological totalizing.

In that way, we think Derrida offers not a method of subverting the tradition, but one whereby the tradition is faithfully read in a spirit of affirmation. Derrida appeals to us to cherish what thinkers such as Plato and Hegel have bequeathed to our culture. But he also cautions against reading them as people who had magically transcended time and place. That, in essence, is what Derrida said every time he wrote about a central figure in the canon of Western thought.

We have made clear why we think that elements of Derrida's political pronouncements are ill-conceived. Indeed, in making those statements, Derrida did become a typical spokesman for what Scruton terms "the culture of repudiation". But in so much else that he wrote and said Derrida repudiated that culture of repudiation. Yes, it is a pity that he wrote so obscurely, and that he imbued his prose with such heavy doses of jargon. That is why he is not considered a philosopher in the traditional sense. Iris Murdoch captured that wonderfully when she wrote:

> [Derrida] is far more like Nietzsche and Freud than like Wittgenstein. He is a remarkable thinker, a great scholar, a brilliant maverick polymath, a pharmakeus. But if thought of as philosophy, the aesthetic requirement of the doctrine tends to exclude sober plodding reflection, slow lucid explanation, simple clear thinking.
>
> (Murdoch 1992: 291)

Murdoch is correct: Derrida did not write soberly, lucidly or simply. But beneath the jargon there is a simple message: philosophy can only go so far in its quest to recollect origins and provide identity with a foundational base. That is not anti-philosophy; rather, it is merely the attempt to make philosophy more honest with itself about its ultimate aspirations. Consequently, Derrida was not in the business of making strong truth-claims. Neither did he aim to build deconstruction into a school of thought. He was simply in the modest business of persuading his readers that understanding who we are is more complicated than philosophy has traditionally presupposed.

That is why Rorty hits the mark when he says that someday "our descendents may wish that Derrida's contemporaries had been able to read him not as a frivolous iconoclast, but rather as a sentimental educator" (1998a: 184). He is a sentimental educator because he takes you by the hand through the labyrinth of texts that constitute the philosophical tradition. In so doing, he schools the reader in the richness of what that canon has to convey. But he also shows how each of those thinkers comprised flesh and blood, and how each of their grand designs was ultimately flawed. That, he instructs, is a sound moral lesson because it forces us to confront our philosophical boundaries.

In the last analysis, therefore, Derrida should be read both as an identity theorist and as a sentimental educator. Approaching his work in that vein will not make reading it any less complex. But it certainly will make it more worthwhile, intriguing and sensible.

Notes

Chapter 1: The catastrophe of memory: identity and mourning

1. For more on the theme of the "catastrophe of memory," see Mark Dooley, "The Catastrophe of Memory: Derrida, Milbank, and the (Im)possibility of Forgiveness", in *Questioning God*, J. D. Caputo, M. Dooley & M. J. Scanlon (eds), 129–49 (Bloomington, IN: Indiana University Press, 2001).
2. The theme of autobiography recurs throughout Derrida's work. See in particular *A Taste for the Secret* (TS), *Monolingualism of the Other* (MO), and *The Ear of the Other* (EO).
3. While Derrida is critical of the attempt to repeat the past as the "same", the notion of repetition as a repetition-with-difference plays an important part in his philosophy of language, as we will see in Chapter 2.
4. Derrida explores the themes of memory and blindness in *Memoirs of the Blind* (MB).
5. This is what Derrida means by "negotiation", which, as we will see in Chapter 4, is central to his ethical and political philosophy.
6. Derrida develops the logic of the gift in detail in *Given Time* (GT) and *The Gift of Death* (GD).
7. For a comprehensive and erudite study on Derrida and Judaism see Gideon Ofrat, *The Jewish Derrida*, Peretz Kidron (trans.) (Syracuse, NY: Syracuse University Press, 2001).
8. We shall return to the themes of mourning and melancholia in our discussion of psychoanalysis in Chapter 3.
9. See R. Rand, "Canons and Metonymies: An Interview with Jacques Derrida", in *Logomachia: The Conflict of the Faculties*, R. Rand (ed.), 197–218 (Lincoln, NE: University of Nebraska Press, 1992), 210.

Chapter 2: Death and *différance*: philosophy and language

1. And as Derrida notes, Plato often has recourse to metaphors of writing to describe speech. Indeed the text of the *Phaedrus* is itself an indictment of writing in writing. And this reliance on writing metaphors recurs at key points throughout Plato's texts, in the *Republic* and the *Timaeus*, for example, where the very origin of the world is conceived of in terms of a "trace" (D: 159).
2. It is interesting to note that not only was Socrates himself born on the sixth day of Thargelia and the ritual of the *pharmakos*, but he was also eventually to play this role in his trial and execution.
3. For detailed comparison of the works of Kierkegaard and Derrida see Mark Dooley, *The*

Politics of Exodus: Kierkegaard's Ethics of Responsibility (New York: Fordham University Press, 2001).

4. See the essay *"Différance"*, in *Margins of Philosophy* (M), 1–27.

5. In the original Hebrew the word "emeth" is written beginning with a silent "aleph": the Latin "A". It is the aleph that is erased from the golem's forehead, and accounts for the difference between life and death.

6. For a developed analysis of Hegel's and Derrida's respective theories of signification see Mark Dooley, "Murder on Moriah: A Paradoxical Representation", *Philosophy Today* 39 (Spring 1995), 67–83.

7. To understand some of the key differences between Derrida and his contemporaries see "Choosing One's Heritage", in *For What Tomorrow ... A Dialogue* (FWT), 1–19, and *The Work of Mourning* (WM).

8. Saussure's *Course in General Linguistics*, W. Baskins (trans.) (New York: Philosophical Library, 1959) was first published posthumously in 1916.

9. See Derrida's discussions of Saussure in his interview with Julia Kristeva in *Positions* (P), 15–36, and his detailed study of linguistics and semiology in *Of Grammatology* (OG).

10. It is important to note that while Saussure is a vital influence for Derrida, he never considered himself a part of the structuralist movement. In fact, Derrida argues that deconstruction is an attempt to *challenge* the basic presuppositions of structuralism: "The first step for me, in the approach to what I proposed to call deconstruction, was a putting into question of the authority of linguistics, of logocentrism. And this, accordingly, was a protest against the 'linguistic turn,' which under the name of structuralism, was already well on its way ... Deconstruction was inscribed in the 'linguistic turn,' when it was in fact a protest against linguistics!" (TS: 76). See also "Structure, Sign and Play in the Discourse of the Human Sciences", in *Writing and Difference* (WD), 278–93.

11. See in particular the "Afterword" to *Limited Inc* (LI), 146.

12. "Through the values of 'conventionality,' 'correctness,' and 'completeness' that intervene in the definition, we necessarily again find those of an exhaustively definable context, of a free consciousness present for the totality of the operation, of an absolutely full meaning that is master of itself: the teleological jurisdiction of a total field whose *intention* remains the organizing center ..." (M: 323).

13. On the relationship between deconstruction and literary criticism see Derrida's comments in "Deconstruction and the Other" (DO), 155.

14. See John Searle, "The World Turned Upside Down", in *Working Through Derrida*, Gary B. Madison (ed.), 170–88 (Evanston, IL: Northwestern University Press, 1993).

15. Derrida himself, however, *did* reply to each of Searle's points in painstaking detail, so we refer the interested reader to the original texts and Derrida's lengthy response in *Limited Inc.* (LI).

16. This basic misreading guides the arguments of Searle's article in the *New York Review of Books*, where he claims that, according to Derrida, "It turns out that speech is really a form of writing, understanding a form of misunderstanding", and that Derrida endeavours "to show that writing is really prior, that speech is really a form of writing" (Searle, "The World Turned Upside Down", 171–4).

17. For more on the topic of "relativism" see Derrida's comments in "Hospitality, Justice and Responsibility" (H), 78–9.

18. See in particular "Deconstruction and the Other" (DO), 154.

19. Derrida discusses this affair in "*Honoris Causa*: 'This is *also* extremely funny'", in *Points ... Interviews, 1974–94* (P), 399–421.

20. See, for example, Samuel C. Wheeler III, *Deconstruction as Analytic Philosophy* (Stanford, CA: Stanford University Press, 2000).

21. Wheeler mistakenly attributes an "indeterminacy of meaning" position to Derrida in an attempt to align him closer to Quine. But Derrida has never advocated the "inde-

terminacy of meaning". See Wheeler, *Deconstruction as Analytic Philosophy*, Chap 1, "Indeterminacy of French Interpretation".

Chapter 3: Repetition and post cards: psychoanalysis and phenomenology

1. Of course, Freud has a lot to say about mourning, and Derrida owes much of his own thoughts on the matter to the work of psychoanalysis. But, as we shall see, they have differing opinions as to what mourning consists in.
2. Derrida has written extensively on Freud, but we refer the reader to the following texts in particular: *The Post Card* (P); *Archive Fever* (AF); *Resistances of Psychoanalysis* (Res); and "Freud and the Scene of Writing", in *Writing and Difference* (WD), 196–231. See also his interview with Elisabeth Roudinseco, "In Praise of Psychoanalysis", in *For What Tomorrow* (FWT), 166–96.
3. Indeed, Freud often describes the psyche in terms of a writing machine: that consciousness is an effect of a system of deferrals and differences of libidinal forces. See Derrida, "Freud and the Scene of Writing".
4. Derrida discusses these differences in "The Double Session", in *Dissemination* (D), 173–359.
5. So Derrida desires *both* to keep (like the melancholic) *and* let go (like Freud), while reducing the work of mourning to *neither* one *nor* the other.
6. Derrida's primary texts on Husserl are *The Problem of Genesis in Husserl's Philosophy* (Chicago, IL: University of Chicago Press, 2003); *Edmund Husserl's Origin of Geometry: An Introduction* (Lincoln, NE: University of Nebraska Press, 1989); *Speech and Phenomena and Other Essays on Husserl's Theory of Signs* (SP); and "Genesis and Structure in Husserl's Phenomenology", in *Writing and Difference* (WD), 154–68. See also Leonard Lawlor, *Derrida and Husserl: The Basic Problem of Phenomenology* (Bloomington, IN: Indiana University Press, 2002).
7. For a detailed discussion of the role of repetition in Husserl, Derrida and Heidegger, see John D. Caputo, *Radical Hermeneutics: Repetition, Deconstruction and the Hermeneutic Project* (Bloomington, IN: Indiana University Press, 1987).
8. See Caputo, *Radical Hermeneutics*, 43–7.
9. Heidegger is a constant presence in Derrida's work, but see in particular "The Ends of Man" in *Margins of Philosophy* (M), 109–36; *Mémoires: For Paul de Man* (MdP); *Aporias* (A); and *Of Spirit: Heidegger and the Question* (OS).
10. See Derrida's interview with Elisabeth Roudinesco, "Of the Anti-Semitism to Come", in *For What Tomorrow* (FWT), 106–38.

Chapter 4: The risks of negotiation: ethics and politics

1. So while anyone can pontificate about the guilt or innocence of the defendant from our previous example, only the judge lays her neck on the line and, enduring the aporia of the undecidable, commits to a distinction and a decision.
2. "That is why Kierkegaard's *Fear and Trembling* is a major text, however we interpret it. It is the moment when the general categories have to be overcome, when I am alone facing a decision" (H: 67).
3. Derrida, "Violence and Metaphysics", in *Writing and Difference* (WD), 79–153.
4. See also Mark Dooley, "A Civic Religion of Social Hope: A Reply to Simon Critchley", *Philosophy and Social Criticism* 27(5) (2001), 35–58.
5. The whole point of the deconstruction of the *logos*, the whole point of the claim that "there is nothing outside the text", is not to affirm the "nothing": to simply replace the substantial essentialisms of the tradition with an empty moralizing that absolves itself

of the responsibility to make decisions altogether. When Derrida says there is nothing outside the text, he means that when we are faced with a decision, we cannot appeal to some extraneous law or source of authority to dictate to us what we should do. But this does not mean we cannot make decisions. It just means that we have to take responsibility for these decisions *ourselves*. Like Abraham, we all have to affirm the risks and aporias of the undecidable, and assume the urgency of a concrete decision. This simple point is often overlooked by the proponents of postmodernism.

6. For more on this theme see "Politics of Difference", in *For What Tomorrow* (FWT), 20–32.

7. Which is why, in *Specters of Marx* (SM), Derrida again attempts to distance himself from Heidegger. Whereas Derrida thinks justice (*dike*) in terms of dis-adjustment, Heidegger thinks justice "on the basis of Being as presence (*als Anwesen*), that is, as always in Heidegger, on the basis of the *logos* or *legein*, a force of gathering (*Versammlung*) and accord" (FWT: 81).

8. Much of what Habermas has to say about Derrida in his *The Philosophical Discourse of Modernity*, Frederick G. Lawrence (trans.) (Cambridge, MA: MIT Press, 1987) relies on the types of misreadings and misconceptions that we dealt with in Chapter 2, and that Derrida himself dealt with in great detail in *Limited Inc.* (see in particular a lengthy footnote, LI: 156–7). For a more fruitful analysis of the debate between Derrida and Habermas see Lasse Thomassen (ed.), *The Derrida–Habermas Reader* (Chicago, IL: University of Chicago Press, 2006).

9. See Jacques Derrida and Mustapha Tlili (eds), *For Nelson Mandela* (New York: Seaver Books, 1987), 13–42. On the Prague affair see *Points … Interviews 1974–94* (P), 128–9.

10. On Algeria see "Taking Sides for Algeria", in *Negotiations: Interventions and Interviews, 1971–2001* (N), 117–24 and *Rogues: Two Essays on Reason* (R), 28–41. On the Israel–Palestine question see "Interpretations at War: Kant, the Jew, the German", in *Acts of Religion*, Gil Anidjar (ed.), 135–88 (New York: Routledge, 2002). On the death penalty see "Death Penalties", in *For What Tomorrow* (FWT), 139–65. On animal rights see "Violence Against Animals", in *For What Tomorrow* (FWT), 62–76.

11. See Jacques Derrida and Peter Pericles Trifonas, *Ethics, Institutions and the Right to Philosophy* (Lanham, MD: Rowman & Littlefield, 2002) and Derrida, *Right To Philosophy I: Who's Afraid of Philosophy?*, Jan Plug (trans.) (Stanford, CA: Stanford University Press, 2002) and *Right To Philosophy II: Eyes of the University*, Jan Plug (trans.) (Stanford, CA: Stanford University Press, 2004).

12. "Political analysis must be begun again, adjusted, refined in each situation, taking into account its greatest complexity, the forces or the current that one is plugging into, or attempting to plug into" (P: 33).

13. For a criticism of Derrida's reading of Marx see Richard Rorty, "A Spectre is Haunting the Intellectuals: Derrida on Marx", in *Philosophy and Social Hope*, 210–22 (New York: Penguin, 1999).

14. "[D]emocracy protects itself and maintains itself precisely by limiting and threatening itself" (R: 36).

Afterword

1. A classic example of postmodernist excess is Jean Baudrillard's *Simulacra and Simulation* (Ann Arbor, MI: University of Michigan Press, 1995), or his *The Gulf War Did Not Take Place* (Bloomington, IN: Indiana University Press, 1995).

Further reading

Derrida's texts can be notoriously difficult for the new reader. His work presupposes a familiarity with the history of philosophy that would intimidate many a university professor. But while his written texts can be remarkably dense, in interviews and roundtables Derrida could be extremely clear, insightful and accessible.

The first port of call for the new reader should be his interview with Richard Kearney, "Deconstruction and the Other", in Richard Kearney, *Debates in Continental Philosophy: Conversations with Contemporary Thinkers* (New York: Fordham University Press, 2004); his extended interviews with Maurizio Ferraris and Gianni Vattimo in Jacques Derrida and Maurizio Ferraris, *A Taste for the Secret*, Giacoma Donis (trans.) (Cambridge: Polity, 2002); and his collection of interviews with Elisabeth Roudinesco in Jacques Derrida and Elisabeth Roudinesco, *For What Tomorrow ... A Dialogue*, Jeff Fort (trans.) (Stanford, CA: Stanford University Press, 2004). For the slightly more advanced reader we also recommend Elisabeth Weber (ed.), *Points ... Interviews, 1974–94*, Peggy Kamuf *et al.* (trans.) (Stanford, CA: Stanford University Press, 1995) and Jacques Derrida and Elisabeth Roudinesco, *Negotiations: Interventions and Interviews, 1971–2001* (Stanford, CA: Stanford University Press, 2002). Two roundtables that are particularly insightful are "The Villanova Roundtable", in John D. Caputo, *Deconstruction in a Nutshell: A Conversation with Jacques Derrida* (New York: Fordham University Press, 1997) and "Hospitality, Justice and Responsibility: A Dialogue with Jacques Derrida", in *Questioning Ethics*, Richard Kearney and Mark Dooley (eds) (London: Routledge, 1999).

For secondary reading we highly recommend Caputo, *Deconstruction in a Nutshell*; Christopher Norris, *Derrida* (Cambridge, MA: Harvard University Press, 1987); and for the more advanced reader, Geoffrey Bennington and Jacques Derrida, *Jacques Derrida* (Chicago, IL: University of Chicago Press, 1993). We also refer the reader to two useful books by Niall Lucy: *Debating Derrida* (Melbourne: Melbourne University Press, 1995) and *A Derrida Dictionary* (Oxford: Blackwell, 2004).

References

Austin, J. L. 1962. *How to do Things with Words*, S. F. Glaser (trans.). Oxford: Oxford University Press.

Baudrillard, J. 1995. *Simulacra and Simulation*. Ann Arbor, MI: University of Michigan Press.

Baudrillard, J. 1995. *The Gulf War Did Not Take Place*. Bloomington, IN: Indiana University Press.

Bennington, G. & J. Derrida 1993. *Jacques Derrida*. Chicago, IL: University of Chicago Press.

Caputo, J. D. 1987. *Radical Hermeneutics: Repetition, Deconstruction and the Hermeneutic Project*. Bloomington, IN: Indiana University Press.

Condillac, E. 1973. *Essai sur l'origine des connaissances humaines*, with an introductory essay by Jacques Derrida. Paris: Galilée.

Davidson, D. 1984. *Inquiries into Truth and Interpretation*. Oxford: Oxford University Press.

Dooley, M. 1995. "Murder on Moriah: A Paradoxical Representation". *Philosophy Today* **39** (Spring), 67–83.

Dooley, M. 2001a. "The Catastrophe of Memory: Derrida, Milbank, and the (Im)possibility of Forgiveness". In *Questioning God*, J. D. Caputo, M. Dooley & M. J. Scanlon (eds), 129–49. Bloomington, IN: Indiana University Press.

Dooley, M. 2001b. "A Civic Religion of Social Hope: A Reply to Simon Critchley". *Philosophy and Social Criticism* **27**(5), 35–58.

Dooley, M. 2001. *The Politics of Exodus: Kierkegaard's Ethics of Responsibility*. New York: Fordham University Press.

Freud, S. 1953–74. *The Standard Edition of the Complete Psychological Works of Sigmund Freud*, J. Strachey (ed.), vols IX–X (1906–07). London: Hogarth.

Freud, S. 1958. "Mourning and Melancholia". Reprinted in *The Standard Edition of the Complete Psychological Works of Sigmund Freud*, J. Strachey (ed.), vol. XIV (1914–16), 243–58. London: Hogarth Press/Institute of Psychoanalysis.

Freud, S. 1961. *Beyond the Pleasure Principle*, J. Strachey (trans.). New York: Norton.

Freud, S. 1999. *The Interpretation of Dreams*, J. Crick (trans.). Oxford: Oxford University Press.

Fukuyama, F. 1992. *The End of History and the Last Man*. New York: Free Press.

Glendinning, S. (ed.) 2001. *Arguing with Derrida*. Oxford: Blackwell.

Habermas, J. 1987. *The Philosophical Discourse of Modernity*, F. G. Lawrence (trans.). Cambridge, MA: MIT Press.

Hegel, G. W. F. [1830] 1991. *The Encyclopedia Logic: Part 1 of the Encyclopaedia of Philo-*

sophical Sciences, T. F. Geraets, W. A. Suchting & H. S. Harris (trans.). Indianapolis, IN: Hackett.

Heidegger, M. 1962. *Being and Time*, J. Macquarrie & E. Robinson (trans.). Oxford: Blackwell.

Heidegger, M. 1968. *What is Called Thinking?* J. G. Gray (trans.). New York: Harper & Row.

Heidegger, M. 1971. *Poetry, Language, Thought*, A. Hofstadter (trans.). New York: Harper & Row.

Husserl, E. 1983. *Ideas Pertaining to a Pure Phenomenology and to a Phenomenological Philosophy*, F. Kersten (trans.). The Hague: Martinus Nijhoff.

Husserl, E. 2001. *The Shorter Logical Investigations*, J. N. Findlay (trans.). London: Routledge.

Kierkegaard, S. 1980. *Stages on Life's Way*, H. V. Hong & E. H. Hong (trans.). Princeton, NJ: Princeton University Press.

Lawlor, L. 2002. *Derrida and Husserl: The Basic Problem of Phenomenology*. Bloomington, IN: Indiana University Press.

Levinas, E. 1969. *Totality and Infinity: An Essay on Exteriority*, A. Lingis (trans.). Pittsburgh, PA: Duquesne University Press.

Murdoch, I. 1992. *Metaphysics As a Guide to Morals*. Harmondsworth: Penguin.

Ofrat, G. 2001. *The Jewish Derrida*, P. Kidron (trans.). Syracuse, NY: Syracuse University Press.

Quine, W. V. O. 1961. "Two Dogmas of Empiricism". In *From a Logical Point of View*, 20–46. Cambridge, MA: Harvard University Press.

Rand, R. 1992. "Canons and Metynomies: An Interview with Derrida". In *Logomachia: The Conflict of the Faculties*, R. Rand (ed.), 197–218. Lincoln, NE: University of Nebraska Press.

Rorty, R. 1996. "On Moral Obligation, Truth, and Common Sense". In *Debating the State of Philosophy: Habermas, Rorty, and Kolokowski*, J. Niznik & J. T. Sanders (eds), 48–51. Westport, CT: Praeger.

Rorty, R. 1998a. *Truth and Progress: Philosophical Papers, Volume 3*. Cambridge: Cambridge University Press.

Rorty, R. 1998b. "Habermas, Derrida, and the Functions of Philosophy". In *Truth and Progress: Philosophical Papers, Volume 3*, 307–26. Cambridge: Cambridge University Press.

Rorty, R. 1999. "A Spectre is Haunting the Intellectuals: Derrida on Marx". In his *Philosophy and Social Hope*, 210–222. New York: Penguin.

Saussure, F. de 1959. *Course in General Linguistics*, W. Baskin (trans.). New York: Philosophical Library.

Scruton, R. 2005. *Modern Culture*. London: Continuum.

Searle, J. 1977. "Reiterating the Differences: A Reply to Derrida". *Glyph* 2, 198–208.

Searle, J. 1993. "The World Turned Upside Down". In *Working Through Derrida*, G. B. Madison (ed.), 170–88. Evanston, IL: Northwestern University Press.

Sellars, W. 1997. *Empiricism and the Philosophy of Mind*. Cambridge, MA: Harvard University Press.

Thomassen, L. (ed.) 2006. *The Derrida–Habermas Reader*. Chicago, IL: University of Chicago Press.

Wheeler, S. C. 2000. *Deconstruction as Analytic Philosophy*. Stanford, CA: Stanford University Press.

Wittgenstein, L. 2002. *Tractatus Logico-Philosophicus*, D. F. Pears & B. F. McGuiness (trans.). London: Routledge.

Index

161